TOWARD FULLNESS OF LIFE

Books by
Suzanne de Dietrich

Published by The Westminster Press

THE WITNESSING COMMUNITY:
THE BIBLICAL RECORD OF GOD'S PURPOSE

GOD'S UNFOLDING PURPOSE:
A GUIDE TO THE STUDY OF THE BIBLE

FREE MEN:
MEDITATIONS ON THE BIBLE TODAY

TOWARD FULLNESS OF LIFE:
STUDIES IN THE LETTER OF PAUL
TO THE PHILIPPIANS

TOWARD FULLNESS OF LIFE

STUDIES IN
THE LETTER OF PAUL
TO THE PHILIPPIANS

By
Suzanne de Dietrich

THE WESTMINSTER PRESS

PHILADELPHIA

PUBLISHED BY THE WESTMINSTER PRESS®
PHILADELPHIA, PENNSYLVANIA

PRINTED IN THE UNITED STATES OF AMERICA

CONTENTS

Chapter 1. A CHURCH IS BORN IN PHILIPPI
      (*Acts, ch. 16*) 7

Chapter 2. "SLAVES" AND "SAINTS"
      (*Phil. 1: 1-2*) 14

Chapter 3. WHAT IS "COMPLETION"?
      (*Phil. 1: 3-11*) 21

Chapter 4. "TO LIVE IS CHRIST"
      (*Phil. 1: 12-26*) 30

Chapter 5. STANDING FIRM
      (*Phil. 1: 27 to 2: 4*) 38

Chapter 6. "OBEDIENT UNTO DEATH"
      (*Phil. 2: 5-11*) 45

Chapter 7. SHINING AS LIGHTS IN THE WORLD
      (*Phil. 2: 12-18*) 53

Chapter 8. FELLOW WORKERS IN THE LORD
      (*Phil. 2: 19 to 3: 1*) 61

Chapter 9. IN THE POWER OF HIS RESURRECTION
      (*Phil. 3: 2-11*) 66

Chapter 10. RUNNING THE RACE
      (*Phil. 3: 12 to 4: 1*) 74

Chapter 11. THE PEACE OF GOD
      (*Phil. 4: 2-9*) 80

Chapter 12. FREEDOM AND MONEY
      (*Phil. 4: 10-23*) 88

1. A CHURCH IS BORN
IN PHILIPPI

(*Acts, ch. 16*)

THE LETTER is written by a prisoner to a church he loves as a father would his child. It sounds like a farewell letter, and it is one of the warmest and liveliest of all Paul's letters.

The study of this letter raises in our minds a few preliminary questions:

Who were these Philippians? What do we know of their background; of Paul's first contacts with them?

What further contacts had been maintained between Paul and this church?

When, from where, and in what circumstances was this letter written? Is it a unit? What was its purpose?

Paul Comes to Philippi

Philippi was a Roman stronghold on the Egnatian Way, the highroad leading from Rome to Asia. It lay about ten miles inland from Neapolis. It was a city with a past. At first it was a tiny Thracian village; then Philip II of Macedonia settled it and fortified it about 357 B.C. It became famous three centuries later as the battlefield between the ambitious generals, Anthony and Octavian, and the Republican leaders, Brutus and Cassius. Out of this victory, the Roman Empire was born. Later the city became a colony endowed with certain privileges.

From a religious point of view, Philippi was a city of many traditions. It was a meeting place of East and West, of ancient Thracian mystery cults and Latin rites, among them the cult of the emperor. "Brotherhoods," or "burial clubs," seem to have been particularly popular. The cult of the dead was held in honor, as it still is today in many parts of Africa and Asia.

We can imagine the apostle Paul and his companions walking on the Egnatian Way toward the unknown city which was to be their first stop on European soil. The book of The Acts tells us about the circumstances of this new missionary enterprise. Paul, in a dream, had heard the call of a Macedonian beseeching him: *"Come over to Macedonia and help us."* We have the story from one of Paul's companions, who went to Macedonia with him and gave a lively account of the proceedings. (See the "we" references in The Acts, which start at *ch. 16: 10.*) One can almost see the four men searching the city for some Jewish colony to which they could announce the good news of Christ (Paul always started that way, whenever possible); and finding, after several days, some women celebrating the Sabbath on the riverside. The Jewish colony must have been tiny, as it had no synagogue. The first convert was a businesswoman and "a worshiper of God," that is, one who accepted the Jewish faith in the one God, without submitting to all requirements of Jewish law. She was a dealer in purples from the city of Thyatira, in Lydia, famous for this trade. We hear that the whole household was baptized and that the apostles stayed with them.

A conflict with town authorities broke out in Philippi when Paul silenced a girl who was earning money for her master by soothsaying. The apostles were charged at once with sedition. The owner of the girl knew how to excite a crowd. He played on its anti-Semitic feelings! "These men are Jews and they are disturbing our city. They advocate customs which it is not lawful for us Romans to accept or practice." (Vs. 20-21.)

Nothing is easier than to start a mob shouting and rioting by playing on its nationalistic or religious feelings. The master of the girl got an immediate hearing. The magistrates had Paul and Silas flogged and thrown in jail. The book of The Acts then tells of a marvelous deliverance during the night. But according to Paul's own testimony, the hardships suffered had been great (I Thess. 2: 1-2), and he and his companions had to leave the city. What happened to the newly baptized Christians who were left behind we are not told. It can be presumed that to hold to their confession required courage and depth of conviction. In his letter to them, Paul mentions the fact that they too have had to suffer for Christ. (Phil. 1: 29-30.)

The story of this first visit to Philippi has a message for us. First, the foundation of the church began with the conversion of *one woman*. Paul spoke, but it was God who opened the heart of Lydia so that she listened and believed. Secondly, the gospel, when duly preached, is bound to stir *some trouble*. A day comes when it threatens deep-seated prejudices or vested interests.

Far Away, Yet Still Close

Paul's first visit to Philippi may be dated with sufficient accuracy in about A. D. 49 or 50. We know that he reached Corinth in A. D. 50. We are told that he stayed there for a year and six months (Acts 18: 11), then sailed for Syria, and started visiting the churches of Asia Minor. After that he stayed for two years in Ephesus. This means that five or six years had gone by before he was able to visit Macedonia again. (*Ch. 20: 1-6.*) His first visit had lasted perhaps a few weeks or a few months at the most. And yet, the foundations of a church had been laid, and a bond of fellowship had been created that no distance could break.

What is the secret of Paul's ministry, that the seed cast in foreign ground should bear such rich and lasting fruit? We cannot help thinking of our modern missions and the long time needed before young churches overseas became independent and self-sufficient. One might answer that those days were exceptional times, that the apostolic church was blessed with an outpouring of the Holy Spirit, and that Paul was a man whose preaching was a "demonstration of the Spirit and power" (*I Cor. 2: 4; I Thess. 2: 13*). But has our faith in the power of the Holy Spirit weakened? The apostle Paul's trust did not rest on human strength. Its frailty he knew all too well. It rested in the power of *God's Word.* He could say in full faith that "he who began a good work in you will bring it to completion" (*Phil. 1: 6; I Thess. 5: 24*).

Furthermore, Paul was a man of prayer. He carried in his heart with a fatherly concern the churches he had founded. At the same time, by his trust in God's work in them, he led them quickly to maturity.

Then, of course, even when far away, Paul kept in touch through his letters. When a serious problem arose and Paul was not available, a trusted colleague was sent. We are told with what anxiety the apostle awaited his return. Paul had not only a great mind, but also a burning heart. One of the chief characteristics of his letters is their human warmth. Far or near, he was standing by his churches, and they knew it.

The Letter Itself

Our third question was: When, from where, and in what circumstances was the letter to the Philippians written? No one today seriously questions Paul's authorship of this letter. The tradition is that it was written from Rome, during Paul's first captivity there (the one mentioned in *Acts 28: 16-31*). We can gather from this chapter that Paul had a soldier constantly guarding him, but that he was rather free in his movements and could go on preaching the gospel. This situation corresponds well with what we can gather from the letter itself. The apostle is in custody, awaiting a trial, the issue of which is uncertain. He wants to strengthen the church and prepare her for the worst, at the same time avoiding undue alarm.

The traditional view that the letter was written from Rome in the years A.D. 60-62, however, raises some problems. The main argument against Rome as the place of writing is the *distance*. It took about six weeks to travel from Rome to Philippi, and it is not easy to imagine messengers like Epaphroditus and Timothy undertaking such a voyage and returning soon after (*Phil. 2: 19-25*). Another argument against Rome is that this letter seems to imply that Paul had not visited the church since its foundation. We know through the book of The Acts that he went at least once, and probably twice, to Macedonia and Greece after his stay in Ephesus (*Acts 19: 21-22; 20: 1-3*). We also know that he sent Timothy ahead. (*I Cor. 4: 17; 16: 5-11.*) The violent outburst against the Judaizers (*Phil., ch. 3*) does not seem to fit in with the years 60 and onward as it would at an earlier date. Therefore, a number of scholars have come to believe that the letter must have been written from Ephesus in the

years 53-56. The difficulty remains that we know nothing of a long imprisonment in Ephesus! All we know
is that the apostle did run through great dangers
while there. (*Acts 19: 23-41; II Cor. 1: 8-10.*) Caesarea has also been mentioned as a possibility, Paul
having spent two years in jail there. But this would
solve none of the problems mentioned above.

Other questions have been raised, from what we feel
to be more convincing grounds, with respect to the
unity of the letter. Any reader will be struck by the
fact that the letter seems to come to an end, or close
to an end, after the practical recommendations concerning Epaphroditus (*Phil. 2: 29* or *3: 1a*). The
letter up to that point has sounded peaceful and re-
laxed, the farewell letter of one ready to die. Suddenly
and unexpectedly, the old violence of the fighter re-
appears (*ch. 3*). Dangerous adversaries are threaten-
ing the faith of the church. This new theme goes on
to the end of the chapter; then farewell recommendations start again (*ch. 4: 1-9*). And then, at the very
end of the letter, Paul mentions the gifts that
Epaphroditus has brought. How can we explain these
delayed thanks? Shall we say that the apostle had
more important things in mind? But Epaphroditus'
return to Philippi has already been mentioned in
ch. 2; moreover, news of his illness has reached Philippi (*v. 26*). Surely, the Philippians should have
known at the same time that their gifts, the purpose of
the voyage, had safely reached their destination.

Polycarp, bishop of Smyrna in the second century,
in writing to the Philippians, mentions Paul's letters
to the Philippians as if he knew several of them. As
these letters were read in the churches, one could well
imagine that several fragments finally were put together into one letter. But any reconstruction remains

conjectural. The one suggested by F. W. Beare has much in its favor. He sees in the section from *ch. 3: 2 to ch. 4: 1* a fragment of an earlier letter, and in *ch. 4: 10-20* a letter of thanks sent soon after Epaphroditus' arrival. The main letter, which he would carry with him, would include the first two and the remaining part of *ch. 4.*

Although these suggestions solve some real technical problems, they remain of secondary importance. It is the actual content of the letter that matters now. And those who maintain the unity of the letter as we have it would say that the free way in which the apostle passes from one subject to another is part of the freshness and charm of this epistle. It is from beginning to end an outpouring of the heart. The movement of thought goes constantly from Philippi to Rome and from Rome to Philippi, and reflects the intensity of the concern of each side for the other.

But Christ is the true starting point, the center and the motivating power of Paul and of those to whom he writes. Christ is their life. But "completion" or fullness of life is still ahead "at the day of Christ."

Toward this goal Paul "runs," and urges all to run with him.

2. "SLAVES" AND "SAINTS"

(*Phil. 1: 1-2*)

WHEN WE READ we tend to glance over the "salutations" as a formality of little importance. We may be tempted to do the same when reading a letter of the apostle Paul. In doing so, however, we may miss an important part of the letter, for the very way in which Paul presents himself to his readers is filled with meaning. In unimportant things, Paul follows the customs of his time; the writer is expected to introduce himself, then to name those to whom he writes, then to greet them with some gracious words of appreciation. Paul does all this, but every word takes on unexpected significance. His presentation of himself becomes a profession of faith; the way he addresses his readers, a reminder of their vocation; the salutation, a blessing.

"Paul and Timothy . . ."

Is it not a striking fact that Paul very seldom writes a letter in his name alone? He could do so, being an apostle, even if he were dictating to a secretary! Today, many important church leaders might not readily associate some young colleague's name with their own as they addressed the church. In the early times, there seems to have been a deeper sense of the fundamental corporate nature of the church.

Thus Paul, at the eve of his trial, reminds the church

14

in Philippi that he has a faithful companion at his
side who shares his concern. Timothy is well known in
Philippi. He had lived through the stormy days of
that church's beginnings and had probably visited
it again since. (*Acts 16: 1-3; 18: 5; 19: 21-22; Phil.
2: 19-24.*)

"Slaves of Christ Jesus . . ."

Paul claims no other title than this one, both for
himself and for Timothy. This is rather striking when
we compare this letter with others, such as Galatians
and I Corinthians. In the latter, he stressed his apostolic authority, which was questioned by at least some
elements in the congregation. Here nothing of the kind
is needed, indicating that there is an exceptionally
trustful relationship between Paul and the church.

But why call himself a "slave"? The word has an
unfavorable meaning for us, and most English versions translate it as "servant." But we should remember that the word "slave" sounded just as unpleasant
to Greek ears! The Greeks had a high regard for the
freedom of the citizen, and slaves were thought of as
a kind of subhuman species, with no will of their own,
no power of initiative, utterly dependent on their
masters. Had Paul fallen prey to a concept of Almighty
God as a kind of Oriental despot or slave master? Why
did he choose such a repelling and possibly misleading
term to apply to himself?

That the word is a figure of speech, he himself
acknowledges on another occasion. We are no longer
"slaves of sin," but "children of God," he says. (*Rom.
6: 17-19; 8: 14-16.*) But what Paul wants to stress
here and in Philippians is that he has only *one* Master
and that he is in his Master's hand, whether in life or
in death. Paul sees the whole of mankind as being

enslaved to the powers of evil. Christ has broken this bondage and taken us into his custody at the cost of his life. He died the shameful death of a slave.

In all things Christ did his Father's will, and so must we do his will, not by any outward compulsion, but by the motive of love (*II Cor. 5: 14-15*). We are Christ's, body and soul.

It should also be noted that the same Greek term translated "slave" is used to translate the Hebrew word "servant" in the "servant" passages of the Old Testament (for example, *Isa. 52: 13 to 53: 12*). The vision of the Suffering Servant is before Paul's eyes as he faces the possibility of martyrdom. The apostle's highest ambition is to follow in the footsteps of the Servant of the Lord, whether in life or in death. He is not ashamed of his humiliated condition; this very condition is his title of glory!

Thus, in a single word, "slave," Paul reminds us of what it means to be a Christian: *My life no more my own!*

"To All the Saints in Christ Jesus"

This word "saints" is consistently used by Paul when addressing the churches. Since this word, too, is subject to misunderstanding today, it would be wise to study its exact meaning.

In the Old Testament, every man or thing set apart for the service of God is called "holy." Not only the Temple, but also the vessels of the Temple are holy; not only the priests, but also the people as a whole. "You shall be to me a kingdom of priests and a holy nation." (*Ex. 19: 6.*) "I am the Lord your God; consecrate yourselves therefore, and be holy, for I am holy." (*Lev. 11: 44.*) The words of Exodus are applied in *I Peter 2: 9* to the church:

"But you are a chosen race, a royal priesthood, a holy nation, God's own people, that you may declare the wonderful deeds of him who called you out of darkness into his marvelous light."

How far the members of the churches are from actual "holiness" one can guess when he reads certain pages of Paul's letters to the Corinthians. And yet, even they are called "saints." Neither they nor the Philippians are called "saints" because of some virtue of their own, but only because God has called them, set them apart for his service, sealed them through baptism as belonging to him, and destined them to ultimate glory. God in his mercy considers them already what they are to become; men and women made whole, "sanctified" by the power of the Spirit. As members of the body of Christ, they share in his holiness. He has "sanctified" (or "consecrated") himself for them (*John 17: 19*). They are saints *"in Christ Jesus"* who are at Philippi. God, in his mercy, has chosen to see them not as they are, but *in Christ*, as redeemed by him and called to reflect his image in their lives.

Is not this a glorious anticipation of what we shall be on the last day? Paul's situation, the Philippians' situation, and indeed also our situation, take on real meaning when seen in the light of the final goal toward which we strive.

Special reference is made in Paul's greeting to *"the bishops and deacons."* It is the only salutation in which Paul singles out the leaders of the congregation for mention. Was it because these leaders had been responsible for the sending of Epaphroditus (see *chs. 2: 25; 4: 18*) and for collecting the gifts? We do not know. The bishop (*episkopos*) in secular Greek was an overseer or supervisor, but the word here is in the plural. We should think rather of "elders" than of "bishops" in the sense that word acquired at a later stage in church history. The deacons probably took charge of the poor and may have been involved also in the sending of gifts. We shall hear farther on in Philippians about the generosity of the Macedonian churches.

"Grace to You and Peace . . ."

The *grace* of God in the Old Testament is God himself turning his face toward his children in forgiving mercy. His favor is always undeserved; it is the manifestation of his "steadfast love." He is the Redeemer who blots out our transgressions and makes a new beginning possible. (*Isa. 44: 21-22.*)

In the New Testament the grace of God is manifested in the coming of Jesus Christ. Jesus is the face of God turned toward us. He is the grace and truth of God made flesh. (*John 1: 14-18.*) Therefore, when the apostles speak of the grace and peace of God, they do it in the name of "God our Father and the Lord Jesus Christ." It is in and through Jesus Christ that we are reconciled to God and enjoy his peace.

Peace. No word is more frequently spoken of and printed nowadays than this one. Everybody wants peace on earth, though few seek it. For most people peace means no nuclear war. We may well understand their concern. A realistic view of our world would force us to say that war is raging everywhere, whether open or secret, cold or hot. It takes the form of struggle for prestige between nations, of economic struggle between power groups, with all its consequences of racial strife and class struggle. War is in the factory and in the home. The root of hatred lies deep in the human soul. It is superficial to combat its outward forms only. But it would be equally wrong to reduce the New Testament concept of "peace" to "peace of mind," as some people are so tempted to do!

The Biblical concept of peace is both broader and deeper. In Old Testament language, the concept is one of health and wholeness, both for the individual being and for the community. God's work of salvation is to make whole what is divided and torn, to instill harmony where there is strife, love where there is hatred. The work of Jesus is therefore essentially a work of reconciliation. Our world of broken relationships is to be made whole.

Peace is the Lord's specific gift to those who share the same grace, the same forgiveness, and the same unity in him (see *John 14: 27; 20: 19-26*). He sends his disciples into the world to proclaim and bring his peace. (*Matt. 5: 9.*) The salutation "Peace!" is to become a reality in the life of those who believe in him. (*Luke 10: 5.*) When Paul writes, "Grace to you and peace from God our Father and the Lord Jesus Christ," it is more than a salutation. It is a blessing, *a word with power* that does what it says if received in faith.

Let us now draw together our insights from these words of greeting in Paul's letter by asking the question, "According to these two introductory verses, what does it mean to be a Christian?"

The highest title of honor for an apostle is to be "a slave of Christ," to follow in the footsteps of him who came in the form of a servant and died the death of a slave. *My life no more my own!*

The highest title of honor with which to address a Christian is "saint," thus recognizing him as a member of the family of God, called in Christ and set apart for God's use, and by faith already a member of the holy fellowship of saints.

There is a contrast between the word "slave," which Paul chooses for himself, and the word "saints," which he applies to his fellow Christians. The first word describes the humiliated condition of the Christian on earth; the second, his ultimate goal, the promise of redemption in Jesus Christ.

This salutation, therefore, gives us in a nutshell the whole theme of the letter.

3. WHAT IS "COMPLETION"?

(*Phil. 1: 3-11*)

"I thank my God whenever I think of you . . . ."[1]

THANKFULNESS should be the dominant note of all Christian worship and Christian life! The Jewish liturgies started with God's praise, and so did the early Christian worship. Maybe we have lost something of the awe and wonder that filled the believer of old when he stood before God and thought of his great deeds, of his forbearance and love, and, above all, of his saving power as revealed in Christ.

Paul is never tired of thanking God for every mark of faith and life that he sees in the churches. All his letters begin this way (Galatians excepted, and there were good reasons for such an exception). But there are subtle shades of meaning in the way he gives thanks, and from this we could already guess something of the strong and the weak points of a given church. (Compare, for instance, Philippians or the Thessalonian letters with I and II Corinthians.)

Paul is not of a certain Puritan breed who thinks that we should always start by telling people what is wrong with them! This will be said when necessary at a later stage. With apostolic wisdom, Paul sees,

---

[1] *Phil. 1: 3.* From *The New English Bible, New Testament.* © The Delegates of the Oxford University Press and The Syndics of the Cambridge University Press 1961. Reprinted by permission.

first, the positive elements in the church's life and
. . . thanks God.

In the case of the Macedonian churches, there is
exceptional warmth in his thanksgiving. We know of
no other church to whom he could have said that he
"always" prayed for them "with joy"! What a magnificent tribute from a pastor to his flock!

Why are Paul's prayers so joyful? Because of the
Philippians' *"partnership in the gospel from the first
day until now."* His closeness to the Philippians is
that of fellow soldiers engaged in the same holy battle.
They have been striving and suffering together for
the furtherance of the gospel. They are dedicated to
the same cause. The apostle Paul seems to have been
often a lonely fighter, especially in the latter part of
his life. Here is a church that stands by him, steadfast
in the faith.

How does this companionship manifest itself? We
may presume that the new converts did not have an
altogether easy time after Paul and his fellow workers
were forced to leave their town in great haste (*Acts
16: 39-40*). They have become Christ's witnesses in
Philippi (*Phil. 1: 27-30*), and the tribute that Paul
pays to the Thessalonians is probably also true of
them: "And you became imitators of us and of the
Lord, for you received the word in much affliction,
with joy inspired by the Holy Spirit" (*I Thess. 1: 6*).
We know that the church in Philippi had actively
assisted the apostle with the sending of messengers and
gifts. (*Phil. 4: 15-16.*) Writing to the Corinthians,
Paul pays a magnificent tribute to the churches of
Macedonia: "We want you to know, brethren, about
the grace of God which has been shown in the churches
of Macedonia, for in a severe test of affliction, their
abundance of joy and their extreme poverty have

overflowed in a wealth of liberality on their part. For they gave according to their means, as I can testify, and beyond their means, of their own free will, begging us earnestly for the favor of taking part in the relief of the saints—and this, not as we expected, *but first they gave themselves to the Lord and to us by the will of God.*" (*II Cor. 8: 1-5,* italics added.) The collection mentioned here is one made for the mother church in Jerusalem. But Paul's words show the spirit of those in these churches, including Philippi, who gave first their hearts to the Lord and, *in consequence,* their money for the brethren. Does this mean that the church has attained a state of perfection? Certainly not! Paul's confidence does not rest on what they actually are, but only in God's faithfulness, for he will achieve what he has begun. He will *"bring it to completion."* The steadfastness with which they have stood by in the apostle's days of need is a sign that God is at work among them. But the time of ultimate revelation and fulfillment has not yet come. What Paul means by "completion at the day of Jesus Christ" will become clearer as we study the following verses. Here the main stress is on the faithfulness of God.

Verse 7 explains further why Paul prays with such joy for the Philippians: they partake of *the "grace" given to him.* It seems that Paul has here something more specific in mind than the grace of God shared by all believers. He mentions his imprisonment and the fact that he is able in this very situation to bear testimony to the truth of the gospel. In presenting his defense he "vindicates" the gospel. By their intercession and their active help the Philippians share in Paul's apostolic mission; they partake of the strife and glory of his ministry. He carries them *in his heart.* They are *all* present in his mind, in his prayer, in his concern, just as they share his concern.

Real community is not a matter of feelings. It grows out of a common call and a common goal. What binds the Philippians to Paul is not only that he is the founder of their church, nor their personal affection for him, but their common dedication to the proclamation of the gospel to the nations. This is the unbreakable bond which binds the Philippians, all of them, known or unknown, to Paul and Paul to them. This is God's grace bestowed on them.

In *v. 8,* Paul, in a sudden outburst, confesses his yearning to see the Philippians again. He calls God himself to witness to the depth of this longing. For it is Christ's love for the Philippians that burns in him. *"I long for you in the heart* [literally: "in the bowels!"] *of Christ Jesus!"*

Let us thank God for this touch of human tenderness in the great apostle. He knows the price of visible fellowship. Faith does not make us less human, but rather more. Does not one of the messianic promises say that our hearts of stone will be changed into hearts of flesh? (*Ezek. 11: 19.*) If Paul was such a great founder and builder of churches, was it not because Christ's love was consuming his heart?

"And It Is My Prayer . . ."

From giving thanks Paul now moves to petition. His intercession bears on the love that the members of the church have for one another. He does not question this love. But it should grow in "knowledge and all discernment," or "insight." These words may mean an enlightened knowledge of God's revelation in Christ as over against erroneous doctrines (*Rom. 10: 2*), as well as a deeper understanding of God's will for them, implying tact and discernment in mutual relationship. (See *Col. 1: 9-10*.)

"So that you may approve what is excellent . . . ." (*V. 10*.) The translation does not fully render the Greek words of this verse, which suggests discriminating thought, a testing of existing differences, a putting first of what is essential. Paul does not develop his thought any further at this point. He will do so in *ch. 2*. We can already guess, however, that there is some tension between certain members of the church, which stands as a stumbling block in the way to full unity and fellowship. It is suggested rather than said. Paul is remarkably tactful in his approach, but he knows very well what it is for which he prays!

For the second time he directs the thoughts of his readers to the coming of Christ. He wants them to be "pure and blameless" when the great day comes and filled "with the fruits of righteousness." This is the "completion" for which Paul prays.

The time has come to ask ourselves exactly what this word "completion" means, for this is a fundamental thought in Paul's teaching. The word "completion" implies, first, that something is *done,* and secondly, that something remains *to be done.* Christian life has a starting point and a goal.

Something Is Done

Righteousness is God's gift in Christ. In Biblical terms, the word means a right relationship between God and man and between man and man. We live in a world of broken relationships. The great act of God in Christ is an act of reconciliation. Christ has taken upon himself the plight of mankind and conquered sin and death in our name. In him we have forgiveness and the possibility of a victorious life. So, in Christ,

God, in his mercy, considers us already as "righteous." From this point of view, the cross of Christ marks a decisive, "once-for-all" turning point in the history of mankind. A way from death to life has been opened; a way from servitude to freedom.

The mystery of justification lies in this identification of Christ with us, and we with Christ. He dies our death that we may live his life. This is a central thought in all Paul's teaching. Baptism is the symbolic act by which we die and are raised with him and are incorporated in his body, the church. (*Rom., ch. 6.*)

It is the self-spending love of God in Christ that accomplishes this reconciliation. This fact fills Paul with adoration and wonder. He never stops considering this miracle of grace: "God was in Christ reconciling the world to himself" (*II Cor. 5: 19*). This is *done,* and we should believe it!

Something Remains to Be Done

First of all, the world has to know what God has done for it. This is why Paul relentlessly preaches the gospel. This is why it is all-important for him that the Philippians share in faith and deed in his apostolic work.

Secondly, every church should be a sign among nations that the great reconciliation has taken place. And a church can only be this sign if reconciliation has truly taken place in its own midst. Hence, the ardent prayer that the Philippians' love may grow in knowledge and understanding! This will be developed later in the letter, but it is significant that the apostle's prayer already focuses on this point.

Thirdly, we have to become, as individual members of the body and as a whole, what we already are in faith: "a new creation" in Christ (*II Cor. 5: 17*). The old, self-centered man in us has to die. We are to be "conformed to the image of his Son" (*Rom. 8: 29*). We have to attain fullness of life. This is the work of the Holy Spirit in us.

Here the thought of Paul becomes dialectical, for he affirms at the same time the reality of the change that the Spirit operates in us and the earthly limits of this change.

The Spirit is a *power* at work in God's church. It bears "the fruits of righteousness." (*Phil. 1: 11*.) What this fruit is, Paul tells the Galatians in memorable terms. (*Gal. 5: 22-24*.) And yet, so long as we are in this world, we have only the first fruits of the Spirit. We are saved "in hope." We have to wait "with patience" for our ultimate deliverance. (*Rom. 8: 22-25*.) This is the tension in which the Christian has to live. He works and strives as one whose Lord is risen and has conquered the powers of evil and death. He stands day-by-day under his forgiveness, strengthened and guided by his Spirit. Here lies the secret of his joy. At the same time, he looks forward, in faith and hope, to "the Day of Christ," when the whole of creation will attain to "the glorious liberty of the children of God" (*Rom. 8: 21*).

In Old Testament times, "the day of the Lord" was a day of judgment and wrath, to be awaited in fear and trembling. (*Amos 5: 18-20*.) The messianic hope changes this day to a day of ultimate deliverance. The New Testament retains an earnest note of warning as to this day when all the thoughts of men will be uncovered. Paul wants his churches to prepare for this day, so that they will be found "pure and blameless" (*Phil. 1: 10*).

What does such a sentence as *vs. 9-10* mean, coming from one who does not believe in salvation through good works? We are often confused on this point. Paul knows that all we are and do is by God's grace. (*Ch. 2: 13.*) But God's grace is active, and the work of the Spirit is to build up the body of Christ. We can yield to its impulse or resist it. Paul speaks of the discipline he imposes on his body, of the race he runs to win the prize. (*I Cor. 9: 24-27.*) His is no passive attitude, but a pressing forward toward the goal. (*Phil. 3: 12-16.*) To be pure and blameless is not to be morally perfect, but to take seriously God's grace and mercy and our calling, which necessarily means that we grow in mercy and love in our mutual relationship.

The day of Christ is the great day when his victory over sin and death will become manifested, when death will be no more, when he shall appear in all glory and might. (*I Cor. 15: 20-28; Rev. 21: 1-7.*) Then we shall know as we have been known, love as we have been loved; then our faith will be changed into sight. (*I Cor. 13: 11-12.*) The First Letter of John echoes Paul's expectation when it says: "Beloved, we are God's children now; it does not yet appear what we shall be, but we know that when he appears we shall be like him, for we shall see him as he is. And every one who thus hopes in him purifies himself as he is pure." (*Ch. 3: 2-3.*) This is the great apostolic hope by which the early church lived. It both waited and strove for the day when all will "attain to the unity of the faith and of the knowledge of the Son of God, to mature manhood, to the measure of the stature of the fulness of Christ" (*Eph. 4: 13*).

The "completion at the day of Jesus Christ" that the Christian expects can be no less than the breaking in of the Kingdom of God, that re-creation of all things of which the prophets of old spoke. It may be more difficult for men of the twentieth century to believe in this Second Coming than it was for those of the first century; such a thought does not fit into our present understanding of history and of the universe. But the message of the gospel for all times is that the key to history is God's revelation in Christ, and that in him all human life will find its ultimate fulfillment.

4. "TO LIVE IS CHRIST"

(*Phil. 1: 12-26*)

"I want you to know, brethren . . ."

FOR MOST PRISONERS there is only one question that matters: When will they be released? But Paul does not seem preoccupied with this typical concern. What Paul wants the Philippians "to know" is not the outcome of his trial, the way in which he is treated, and so on. Those more personal questions Epaphroditus can answer when he goes home. They are legitimate and human, but they are not the object of Paul's letter. No! The apostle has, and wants, to share a more important concern: Does his imprisonment impede or forward the spreading of the gospel? This is the *one thing* that really matters from an apostolic point of view!

And here Paul has good news to share with the Philippians. His trial has, so far, served Christ's cause in Rome!

Paul refers to "what has happened to me." Did a hearing take place that allowed him to make a public confession of his faith? Or did his personal witness impress his guardians in such a way that it became a matter for discussion all over the place? We do not know. Anyway, it had become known in the whole praetorium that this was no ordinary prisoner, no political rebel, but a man with such religious convictions that he was ready to die for them. Every member of the imperial guard had had a chance to hear about Christ. A prisoner waiting for his trial, as Paul was, could be allowed to move about, but always chained to a guard. One may be sure that Paul did not miss the opportunity to deliver his message.

Another positive result of Paul's imprisonment was the strengthening of the church at Rome. It may be presumed that the brethren had been somewhat afraid, at first, of the possible repercussions on their own situation of Paul's arrest and transfer to Rome. Now, to the contrary, says Paul, his imprisonment has made them bolder in the proclamation of the gospel.

All this is a matter of rejoicing both for the apostle himself and for those who share his concerns. But Paul avoids painting too glowing a picture of the situation. It has its shadows. The motives of those who preach the gospel with new zeal are not altogether pure (*v. 15*). Some do it, we are told, "from envy and rivalry." What does this mean? We know very little about the situation in the church at Rome at that time. Paul had had no share in its foundation, as his letter to the Romans shows. It seems, from the brief reference to the church in *Acts 28: 14-30*, that he received a hearty welcome on his arrival there. That so strong a personality should evoke "envy" and hostility should not surprise us. We know from his correspondence with other churches, especially from his letters to the Corinthians, that he was a controversial figure. He was much too radical in his insistence on a total allegiance to "Christ alone" to be easily accepted. He was not yet "Saint Paul"!

Little men always find it hard to tolerate great ones, and the church in Rome might have had its share of little men. They would strive to make them-

selves important and to win people's esteem. Such men
would not mind the apostle's being out of the way.
They "proclaim Christ out of partisanship." Their
comments on Paul's preaching must not have been
altogether kind.

But there were others in Rome whose will to proclaim the gospel has been truly kindled by the
apostle's example, and who did so out of genuine love,
because they knew what he had suffered for the sake
of Christ. "What does it matter?" says Paul, in effect.
"Christ is proclaimed; and in that I rejoice!"

It has been said sometimes about this passage that
Paul became more lenient in his old age. This is
scarcely in keeping with all we know of his message
and his character. Paul can be lenient when his own
person is under attack, as is the case here. He will
never be lenient when the truth of the gospel is at
stake. Vigor similar to that shown in the letter to the
Galatians will reappear in *Phil. 3:2*. We must infer
from this that those who preached Christ "from mixed
motives" [1] still preached "Christ" and not some ques-
tionable doctrine of their own.

What one can say about Paul's attitude here is that
he proves to be above personal sensitiveness and resentment. That he was very sensitive whenever some
doubt was thrown on the genuineness of his apostleship we know well from his letter to the Corinthians.
Now, on the threshold of death, people's attitudes
toward him have become a secondary matter, so long
as Christ is proclaimed. This he wants the Philippians
to understand. They, too, must learn to put first things
first. The ego must die if Christ is to grow.

---

[1] From *The New English Bible, New Testament.* © The Delegates
of the Oxford University Press and The Syndics of the Cambridge
University Press 1961. Reprinted by permission.

"Yes, and I Shall Rejoice"

Paul has rejoiced because God is at work in Philippi (*ch. 1: 3-11*). He has rejoiced because God is at work in Rome. Now he looks forward and rejoices because he trusts that God will never fail him. Why this assurance? Paul mentions two reasons: the prayers of the church in Philippi, and "the Spirit of Jesus Christ." Paul claims that he *needs* the prayers of the Philippians to remain steadfast to the end. The members of the body of Christ are closely knit together, and the Lord wants them to intercede for one another, to bear one another up. This is our part in the divine enterprise. To those who stand in supplication before him, God will grant his Spirit. We have already seen in a preceding study that the toils and joys of apostleship are not one man's affairs; they are to be shared also by all those who live by the same grace and faith.

We all know how, in hours of need, we have been sustained by the prayers of friends. This is one of the mysteries and blessings of this fellowship we call "the communion of saints." To the great fighter Paul, the intercession of the churches was an indispensable factor of his ministry.

The second reason for Paul's joyful assurance is the certainty that the Spirit will assist him, so that, whatever the circumstances, he will never be ashamed to confess his faith, but will do so with "full courage." The apostle does not minimize the seriousness of the ordeal to which he might be submitted; he is aware of human weakness. There is no boasting in his attitude. His trust lies in God, who called him and will stand by at the hour of direct need. Paul knows of the Lord's promise to his disciples (*Mark 13: 11*). He has already experienced the unfailing trustworthiness of this promise: Has not God's power manifested itself in the weakness of the flesh all through the hardships of the long ministry? The man who can write to the Philippians, "Now as always Christ will be honored in my body," knows what an ailing, martyred body feels like. It is the man who could write to the Corinthians: "Five times I have received at the hands of the Jews the forty lashes less one. Three times I have been beaten with rods; once I was stoned" (*II Cor. 11: 24-25*). But the same man would say: "But we have this treasure in earthen vessels, to show that the transcendent power belongs to God and not to us. We are afflicted in every way, but not crushed; perplexed, but not driven to despair; persecuted, but not forsaken; struck down, but not destroyed; always carrying in the body the death of Jesus, so that the life of Jesus may also be manifested in our bodies." (*II Cor. 4: 7-10.*)

Paul can say all these things because Christ lives and acts in him, and what he has done, Christ has done through him (*Rom. 15: 18*). His one concern is to glorify Christ, whether through the ongoing witness of his earthly ministry or a martyr's death.

It is in the light of all this that we should understand the next sentence: "For to me to live is Christ, and to die is gain" (*v. 21*).

These words have often been interpreted as expressing the apostle's mystical union with Christ, a oneness that can attain its fulfillment only in the next life. That the longing for such completion is not foreign to the apostle's way of thinking is clear from other passages, such as *II Cor. 5: 6-8*. How could he keep longing for the day when faith will be changed to sight, and we shall know as we have been known? But in the present letter the dominant concern is apostolic witness, and it is from this point of view that Paul wants the Philippians to consider what may happen to him. Because his life belongs to Christ, the real question is whether he will glorify Christ more effectively through life or through death. Offering his life, and sharing thereby in his Lord's sufferings, would be the logical (and probably secretly longed for) conclusion of a life of service. But Paul knows well that the churches still need him. God may want him to stay on; a blessed time of ingathering may lie ahead. So Paul feels torn in his mind between two desires, two forms of service. Finally, he confesses that death would be the better way—not death in itself, but *death with and for Christ* would be the ultimate fulfillment of his apostolic ministry:

"If we have died with him, we shall also live with him;
  If we endure, we shall also reign with him."

(*II Tim. 2: 11.*)

This is what the apostle longs for. But as he says so, a certainty seems to take hold of him that this is not God's will for him. His task in Philippi is not completed. Quite unexpectedly he suddenly declares, "I know that I shall remain and continue with you all."

How does he know? A man of prayer is given at certain moments an inner certainty as to the way God wants him to go. As Paul ardently prays for the Philippians, he is given such a certainty: he will see them again, so that they may be strengthened in their faith and see their prayers answered. They will, through his release, "have ample cause to glory in Christ Jesus." Here again, Christ's glory, not Paul's release, is at the center.

Later in his letter Paul will envisage again the possibility of martyrdom (*ch. 2: 17*). Is it not his concern all through the letter to prepare the church for the possibility of his departure, without provoking undue alarm over a case not yet settled? They should know that he cares for them so deeply that he would choose, for their sake, to go on living, even when personally ready to die. But the dominant purpose throughout the letter is to focus their thoughts, not on Paul, but on Christ. *He* is Paul's life and theirs. Only one thing matters: that Christ be glorified— glorified in Philippi, glorified in Rome, glorified in Paul's life or death. And "glorified" here means revealed as the all-powerful Lord of life and death.

Paul's thoughts are constantly moving from Rome to Philippi, and from Philippi to Rome. But at every point along the road, we meet Christ. Apart from him, all would be meaningless, the strivings of the Philippians and of Paul sitting in jail. With Paul, everything becomes a necessary part of a world-embracing purpose: God's saving power at work among the nations, spreading from the heart of the imperial praetorium to the ends of the earth.

What have we learned from meditating on this passage about what "completion" means? For Paul, as for all men, completion is still a reality of the future, to be prayed for and hoped for. (See *Phil. 3: 12*.) But we can learn from him what it means for a man when Christ has taken hold of him and has become his Lord and Savior in such a way that the man can say: "Christ *is* my life. In other words, my own petty existence has been reduced to naught; my true life is the life I live through faith in him and for him. That he be known by all men is the one thing that matters."

We can see the fruit of the Spirit in the apostle's

life in this passage. First of all, it is apparent in the fact that the dominant note is one of thankfulness and joy. It is no easy thing to be thankful when one sits in jail and the future looks dim, and the brethren make life more difficult by petty intrigues.

Secondly, Paul has learned to put first things first, namely, Christ's Kingship on earth. He is above bitterness and resentment. Think of the little wounds Christians so easily inflict upon one another and that we find so difficult to accept!

Thirdly, Paul has a firm hope, which casts out fear. He is ready for life or death—a hard life and possibly a terrible death.

All this can be summarized by saying that Paul has attained already, to an amazing degree, "the glorious freedom of the children of God," and the secret of this freedom is clearly total dependence on *Christ alone.*

5. STANDING FIRM

(Phil. 1: 27 to 2: 4)

"Only let your manner of life be worthy . . ."

PAUL has expressed the hope that he might be delivered so that he could visit the Philippians again. But this is not his main concern. His concern is that the church in Philippi should "stand firm," whether or not he comes back. His thoughts move back to the community and to the many temptations that threaten its life.

We must keep in mind the situation of these young churches, which were planted by the apostle in an alien world whose way of life and standards presented a constant challenge to that for which the tiny Christian group stood. Such a community could survive only if it stood as one man for the gospel it proclaimed. The terms used remind one, as so often in Paul's writings, of a military squad under attack. Let your life be "ordered." Firmness, unity, striving side-by-side, and fearlessness are the necessary conditions for not being overcome.

Who the opponents were we do not exactly know. What we do know is that the new faith was too absolute in its claims and too demanding in its requirements not to meet with suspicion and open hostility. Was not Paul himself accused of troubling the city in every place he visited?

Calvin comments on *Phil. 1: 28* in this way: "For persecutions are in a manner seals of adoption to the children of God, if they endure them with fortitude and patience: the wicked give a token of their condemnation, because they stumble against a stone by which they shall be bruised to pieces." [1] (Compare *I Peter 2: 6-8.*)

The Christians in Philippi should not be frightened, therefore, because they are under attack. To suffer opposition is a normal situation for a faithful church. To suffer for Christ is regarded by Paul as a privilege, a grace of God. Not that suffering has any virtue in itself and should be searched for, but simply because to follow Christ is to share in his fight against all the powers that hold mankind captive, and this necessarily calls forth their resistance. Jesus warned his followers that they could not be his disciples without bearing their cross. (*Mark 8: 34-38.*) Paul, all through his life, was an exponent of what it means to share in Christ's sufferings. His bold proclamation of the gospel met with such opposition that he had to face slander, flogging, and stoning, and live under constant threat of death. (See *II Cor. 4: 5-12; 11: 24-29; Col. 1: 24.*)

In Philippi as elsewhere, the bold proclamation of the gospel would attract some and call forth the hatred of others. People would be forced to take sides, for or against the new faith. In every missionary situation, the words of Jesus come true: "Do you think that I have come to give peace on earth? No, I tell you, but rather division; for henceforth in one house there will be five divided, three against two and two against three." (*Luke 12: 51-52.*)

---

[1] From *Commentaries on the Epistles of Paul the Apostle to the Philippians, Colossians, and Thessalonians.* Wm. B. Eerdmans Publishing Company. 1948. Used by permission.

There is a great deal of talk about peace going on today. We should remember that Jesus did not welcome any kind of "peace." He denounced "false peace," as did the prophets of old, a truce obtained by covering up evil instead of denouncing it. (*Jer. 6: 14.*) There can be no real peace where there is no justice, no truthful relationships, no knowledge of God's mercy and forgiveness. By denouncing the greed of the rich and the shallowness and hypocrisy of the so-called religious people of his time, Jesus was led to the cross. In rejecting the idols and false securities of their day, the apostles faced martyrdom. Therefore, Paul could consider the fact that the Philippians not only believed in Christ but suffered for his sake as a sign of their election, a gift of God.

The Church Under the Cross

Since Constantine made Christianity the acknowledged religion of the Empire, a kind of pact of "co-existence" has prevailed between church and state. The temptation has been for Christians to accommodate themselves to the ways of the world. Yet every period of history has had its prophets and martyrs, and the missionary enterprise has often been sealed by blood. Today many of the young churches of Asia and Africa are faced with the resurgence of ancient religions. Totalitarian ideologies challenge the Christian faith and try by subtle means to destroy it. But these open attacks may, in the long run, prove less dangerous for the church than the way in which our Western world has left the church in peace because she is considered innocuous! Her ways look so very much like the world's. They are seldom such that the world would feel uncomfortable. Thus, the world gladly leaves the church to its own devices.

Perhaps we are swiftly heading toward a time when costly choices will be necessary if the church is to survive. Our technical civilization has become so involved in material welfare that, to a growing number of people, the very concept of "God" has become irrelevant. Most people seem to live happily in a world of three dimensions, absorbed in day-to-day living. On the other hand, this is also a world in which the struggle for justice and freedom is asserting itself with new force. What does it mean, what should it mean, in such a world, to "suffer for Christ"?

One thing is clear: any kind of conventional Christianity, of lip service, will carry no weight. Only those who stake their whole lives on what they believe will have a chance to be listened to.

To suffer for Christ may mean standing up for our faith in times and places where our convictions will be misunderstood or scoffed at. But it also means, in full loyalty to him, a readiness to listen and to sift and purge our traditions.

To suffer for Christ may mean a readiness to take a stand on the burning issues of the day—on war and peace, on racial equality or social justice. These controversial issues imply costly conflicts for Christians who reject hatred and violence and know of no other weapons than truth.

To suffer for Christ also means to embrace the cause of unity within the body of Christ over against all forms of sectarianism and denominational prestige. It means carrying on our hearts and in our prayers the scandal of our divisions and working to remove them wherever possible.

There are more secret ways of suffering with and for Christ that each community and each individual Christian has to discover: the fight against the enemy in our very midst, in our very soul; the fight for those close and dear to us. Whatever the way God leads us, to love Christ and to try to follow him implies suffering. And the sharing, though in a small way, in our Lord's battle for the liberation of his world is a blessing—the sign of our truly belonging to him.

The Philippians have seen their apostle and his companions beaten and thrown in jail, yet joyful. They have not been spared similar treatment. They are God's spearhead in Philippi by his grace.

"Complete My Joy . . ."

Paul has already stressed the need of being of one mind, united by the same Spirit in order to overcome the outward world. Now he turns to the inner life of the church, and his pleas for unity become so pressing that he seems unable to find enough adequate terms to express his concern. The first verse of *ch. 2* has raised problems of translation and interpretation, which can be seen if one compares different English versions. There is no verb in the original text; the first term can mean "exhortation" or "consolation"; the last words literally mean "bowels and mercies." But the main problem is whether Paul refers in this passage to the Philippians' attachment for him, or to the common life they have already experienced, or to Christ's gifts of consolation, love, and fellowship. All this can be implied in the sentence. But it seems in keeping with Paul's whole approach that his starting point would be Christ. Through his life, death, and resurrection he has revealed the very essence of love; the fellowship of the Philippians is grounded in him, in the Holy Spirit of which they have been made participants. And all of this should manifest itself in the warmth and forbearance in mutual relationships;

in all members of the church striving for the same thing, namely, the completion of their common life in Christ. (*Ch. 2:2.*) Such an achievement would bring the apostolic joy "to the full" (or "fill up my cup of happiness," as in *The New English Bible, New Testament*).

"Do Nothing from Selfishness or Conceit . . ."

Paul finds it necessary to be more specific in the next following verses (*3* and *4*). He thus gives us a glimpse of the real situation. Some members of the church think too highly of themselves; they are self-centered. The religious zeal of new converts can easily make them self-assertive, inclined to spiritual pride. This is not only true of new converts! This leads further to petty jealousies, to comparing one another's merits. Karl Barth quotes a rather striking remark of the old German theologian Bengel: "There is sometimes a certain natural antipathy between the saints!" Is it not a fact that it is sometimes harder to get along with fellow Christians than with non-Christian associates? Is it because one expects more? Is it because of a secret spirit of competition that makes one want to excel over the other? We all know how secret dislikes and petty criticisms can poison the atmosphere of parish life. All of this proves that we have not yet learned what oneness in the Spirit really means. We, as well as the Philippians, should learn humility, to "count others better than [ourselves]."

The advice is not altogether easy to follow! Does humility mean being blind to one's own gifts and to other people's defects? Should we strive to see only their strong sides and our weak ones? Surely such an attitude would be artificial and untrue! But Paul knows the human heart. He knows that we are naturally inclined to see the speck in our brother's eye rather than the log in our own (*Matt. 7: 3*). True humility means standing before God, being aware of one's shortcomings, and living day-by-day by his grace and forgiveness. To know oneself in this light forces one to be merciful toward others and to see them as objects of the same grace and forgiveness. It means to rejoice in their gifts as from God, like our own.

Self-interest and the Interests of Others

Perhaps the word "interests" in *v. 4* is misleading: it makes one think in terms of money. The meaning should rather be "his own right," or "good," or "gift." The old ego is slow in dying. We tend to be more concerned with our own affairs, our own successes, our own rights, than with those of our brother.

The apostle does not ask for the impossible. He does not ask one to be completely detached from one's own "interests," but to be concerned *also* for one's neighbor's. In other words, we should never lose sight of the community as a whole. We should have at heart the common good. Writing to the Corinthians, Paul insists that all gifts should contribute to the building up of the church. (*I Cor. 14: 12.*)

We live in a time of mass movements, in which the individual often feels forlorn and desperately seeks for some kind of true fellowship. A Christian community in which such a fellowship truly exists and permeates all human relationships is the most powerful witness that the living Christ is really present and active among us.

6. "OBEDIENT UNTO DEATH"

(*Phil. 2: 5-11*)

THESE FEW VERSES are among the most beautiful and most discussed texts of the New Testament. Because of their Christological implications, this passage not only becomes a key text in the controversies of the early centuries of the church, but also in the theological discussions of the preceding and present century. How should one understand the statement "he . . . emptied himself," in *v. 7?* How could one who was equal to God, who was God, "empty himself" of his divine attributes and still be God?

It is not our intention to enter into this type of controversy. Much of it has grown out of philosophical concepts about the nature of God drawn from other sources than the Biblical revelation and alien to it. We shall try to cling to the text and to hear the message that Paul himself wanted to convey to his readers. In the heat of theological speculations, the real aim of this passage has often been lost sight of. Paul's concern at this point is *not* to expound a doctrine, but to remind the church of the nature of her calling as Christ's body, meant to conform to him who came as a servant. In other words, his aim is essentially *practical*.

Something should be said here about the literary problem raised by *vs. 6-11*. Most scholars today believe that this passage is an ancient Christian hymn.

Its structure is rhythmical, according to the rules of Hebrew poetry. Attempts have been made by German scholars to reconstruct the hymn in two strophes, or six stanzas of three verses each. Of course, this cannot be fully rendered in translation.[1] The words "even death on a cross" break the rhythm and may be an addition by Paul himself. If this hymn is a quotation, the fact that the apostle uses it means that he agrees with its content as an accepted and well-known statement of faith.

"Have This Mind . . ."

Following these preliminary remarks, let us now look more closely at the text itself:

Verse 5 links what has been said in the preceding verses to what follows: "Have this mind among yourselves, which you have in Christ Jesus," or, "Let this be the disposition that governs in your common life, as is fitting in Christ Jesus," [1] or still more freely, "Let your bearing towards one another arise out of your life in Christ Jesus." [2] The obscurity of the Greek sentence forces one to interpret the meaning somewhat. Paul has urged the Philippians to strive toward the same goal in mutual forbearance and humility. Now he goes a step farther: he is going to remind them what it means for a community to be "in Christ."

This is a Pauline expression which comes up so frequently in Paul's letters that we should dwell a while on its meaning. It describes, not some mystical

---

[1] See *A Commentary on the Epistle to the Philippians,* by F. W. Beare. Harper & Row, Publishers, Inc. Copyright © 1959 by Francis Wright Beare.

[2] From *The New English Bible, New Testament.* © The Delegates of the Oxford University Press and The Syndics of the Cambridge University Press 1961. Reprinted by permission.

experience, but, rather, a new state of being, a new form of existence, the condition of life of those who, through baptism, have been made participants in Christ's death and victory. They have buried the old self with all its claims and pretenses. (*Rom. 6: 3-14.*) Christ is not seen in this passage as a model that we should imitate, but as a Savior who redeems us from sin and death, from the self-assertive kind of life we had been leading before. Of course, this means that, by the power of the Holy Spirit at work in us, we shall be conformed unto him, grow into his likeness. (*Rom. 8: 29.*)

But who is he, in the likeness of whom we are to be shaped? He is the One who chose to come in the form of a servant, who died the death of a slave.

The Philippians are now to contemplate their Lord and Master and to ponder the mystery of his freely consented self-abasement. He who humbled himself is the One whom God has lifted up to the highest place. How could one know that and remain self-assertive?

The Preexistent Christ

Let us look more closely now at *Phil. 2: 5-8:*

"Christ Jesus, who, though he was in the form of God, did not count equality with God a thing to be grasped, but emptied himself, taking the form of a servant, being born in the likeness of men. And being found in human form he humbled himself and became obedient unto death, even death on a cross."

F. W. Beare and other contemporary scholars suggest that the theme of the descent of the Redeemer from heaven to the world of men and to the realm of the dead and his following ascent may have its origin in a pagan myth, possibly Iranian. This seems to us an unwarranted supposition. A similarity of language does not necessarily mean an identity of concepts. The Book of Daniel (*ch. 7: 13-14*) and the apocryphal Jewish Book of Enoch show that a strong tradition existed in Jewry concerning the Son of Man, conceived as a preexistent, heavenly being who was to come at the end of time and judge the world. In the Gospels we find Jesus applying this title to himself. That Paul believed in the preexistence of Jesus Christ seems evident from other passages of his letters, such as *I Cor. 8: 6:* "Yet for us there is one God, the Father, from whom are all things and for whom we exist, and one Lord, Jesus Christ, through whom are all things and through whom we exist." In *I Cor. 15: 47-48* Paul calls Jesus "the man of heaven," in contrast with Adam, "the man of dust." In *II Cor. 8: 9* he writes: "For you know the grace of our Lord Jesus Christ, that though he was rich, yet for your sake he became poor, so that by his poverty you might become rich." The cosmic role of Christ stated in *I Cor. 8: 6* is further developed in the letters to the Colossians and to the Ephesians. The belief in Christ's preexistence is stated not only in Paul's letters but in I Peter, in Hebrews, and, of course, in John's Gospel. It is an article of faith for the apostolic church in the second half of the first century. The merging of the two figures of the Son of Man of Daniel coming in glory at the end of time, and of the Suffering Servant of *Isa., ch. 53,* offering himself for the redemption of men, seems to go back to Jesus himself.

All texts we have quoted affirm the absolute sovereignty of God and the subordination of Christ: He offers his life freely to do the Father's will. It is the Father who raises him up and gives him dominion over heaven and earth.

Let us now come back to the wording of *Phil. 2: 6-7.*
What does it mean that Jesus was "in the form of God,
. . . in the form of a slave"? It seems that Paul does
not oppose here two "forms" of being, but, rather,
two conditions of existence. Christ left the heavenly
realm, implying full and free communion with God,
to submit himself to the earthly condition of man,
with the limitations that this condition implies, in a
world marked by sin and death. To redeem mankind,
he accepted a share in its plight.

"The Form of a Servant . . ."

The story of the first man who did snatch at equality with God is probably in the writer's mind. (*Gen.
3: 5.*) Christ's movement is exactly the reverse of that
of the first man. He could have claimed the pre-
rogatives of Sonship, but he stripped himself of his
dignity as the Son to live the life of an earthly man.
We are reminded here of the temptation story, "If you
are the Son of God . . .," and Jesus' threefold answer.
(*Matt. 4: 1-10.*) We are reminded of the day when
the crowd wanted him to be king, and Jesus went off
to the mountains (*John 6: 15*); of that other day,
when he rebuked Peter severely for not believing that
the Son of Man should suffer and die. (*Mark 8:
32-33*).

The Gospels show quite clearly that the choice was
a firm and deliberate one, but that Jesus did not face
without an inward struggle the vocation of Messiah-
ship, the way of the Suffering Servant, the horror of
death. Is it not the bitter reality of this struggle which
conveys to his "obedience unto death" its depth of
meaning? All through his ministry it is in his total
submission to the Father's will that he manifests the
reality of his Sonship. To do this will is the motivation

underlying every one of his words and actions, and this obedience is to be the touchstone by which he will measure his followers (*Mark 3: 33-35*). His obedience culminates in the cry of Gethsemane, "Not what I will, but what thou wilt" (*Mark 14: 36*). The Letter to the Hebrews sees the Lord's whole life as a fulfillment of words from *Ps. 40:* "Lo, I have come to do thy will, O God" (*Heb. 10: 5-10*). "Although he was a Son, he learned obedience through what he suffered; and being made perfect he became the source of eternal salvation to all who obey him." (*Ch. 5: 8.*)

The Fourth Gospel, whose witnesses have "seen his glory" under the veil of flesh, is the most insistent on the total dependence of the Son upon the Father: "My food is to do the will of him who sent me, and to accomplish his work" (*John 4: 34*). Indeed, it is in this perfect oneness of will and purpose of the Son with the Father, in the free offering of his life, that his divinity manifests itself. (*John 10: 17-18.*) His self-abasement *is* his glory, because it reflects as nothing else could do the very nature of God, his self-spending love.

Christ's obedience is an obedience unto death, "even *death on a cross.*" Paul purposely adds these words. It is the kind of death to which the Romans submitted the slaves, therefore the most shameful of all. The Jewish tradition regarded being hanged on a tree as a sign that God's curse was on the man. (See *Deut. 21: 23; Gal. 3: 13.*) The humiliation and rejection of the Son of God could not have been carried farther. He has taken upon himself the curse befalling mankind. The meaning of the cross is expounded by Paul in other letters. Here he only needs to remind the Philippians of the fact and of its bearing on their situation. Who could sit on a pedestal while claiming to be the servant of this *Servant?* This verse reminds us of our Lord's saying to his disciples:

"Whoever would be first among you must be slave of all. For the Son of man also came not to be served but to serve, and to give his life as ransom for many." (*Mark 10: 44-45;* see *Luke 22: 24-27.*)

"Therefore God Has Highly Exalted Him . . ."

In his humiliation and death, the initiative belonged to Christ. His being exalted is an act of *God.* He who died the death of a slave is made Lord of all. (*Phil. 2: 9-10.*)

That God puts down the mighty from their thrones and exalts those of low degree is a recurring thought of The Psalms. It appears in Luke's Gospel in Mary's Song. (*Ch. 1: 52.*) God is with the humble of heart This is a reminder to the Philippians that the way to glory is open to the meek and lowly.

God bestows on Jesus "the name which is above every name, that at the name of Jesus every knee should bow, in heaven and on earth and under the earth, and every tongue confess that Jesus Christ is Lord, to the glory of God the Father."

There is in these verses in Philippians an echo of *Isa. 45: 23:*

"To me every knee shall bow,
every tongue shall swear."

What Isaiah puts in the mouth of God is now said of the Son. God remains the sovereign God, "For I am God, and there is no other" (*v. 22*). But he has delegated his authority to the Son. Here again Paul contents himself with an affirmation of faith. Christ is

Lord. All power has been entrusted to him. Paul's aim here is to stress the contrast between Christ's humiliation and his present glory, not to develop a theological theme.

The role of Christ as King and Judge in relation to his role as Mediator is clearly developed in *I Cor. 15: 20-28; Col. 1: 15-20;* and *2: 15.* The powers that held humanity captive have been conquered by him— "nailed to his cross." Christ's rule is shown as extending beyond mankind to all the angelic or demonic powers (cf. the "principalities and powers" of *Col. 1: 16,* which, according to the concepts of that time, filled and governed the universe). Such a thought is somewhat foreign to our present way of thinking. But do we not see demonic forces at work in our own day? The certainty expressed here is that all these adverse forces have assailed Jesus Christ in his ultimate fight on the cross and have been overcome. Although our unredeemed world still stands in the grip of all the powers that be, their ultimate defeat is assured. The apostolic faith is that Christ's victory will be revealed on the Last Day. Then every knee will bow and every tongue will confess the Lordship of the Crucified; God's victory over a sinful world has been won on a cross. His unlimited, sacrificial love, revealed in the self-offering of the Suffering Servant, is the only power that could break the deadly circle of sin and death that enslaves man.

The will to dominate, rather than to serve, poisons many relationships today: those between the sexes, as well as between the nations and races. The church itself is not free from this deep-rooted human will to power. Paul's message comes to us as a challenge. It points us to the way of humility and obedience as the only way to peace and salvation.

7. SHINING AS LIGHTS
IN THE WORLD

(Phil. 2: 12-18)

Paul now returns to the exhortations he started in *vs. 1-5* of *ch. 2*. But a new light has been projected on the whole situation. The Servant-King has been lifted up before the eyes of the Philippians, in all his humility and majesty and sovereign authority, all flowing from his relentless obedience.

"Therefore, My Beloved . . ."

The recommendations that follow sound like a farewell message of the apostle to his beloved church. Some scholars think that Paul has in mind the farewell message of Moses to the Israelites in *Deut. 31: 25 to 32: 5*. This is an interesting thought, yet to us not entirely convincing. One as rooted in the Scriptures as Paul was would naturally use similar words and phrases. The point is that whereas Moses sees in his people nothing but past disobedience, Paul can say, "As you have always obeyed." Moses describes the Israelites as a "perverse and crooked generation," but Paul applies this word to the outside world, in which the Philippians are to shine like stars. The dark view Moses takes of the future is in striking contrast to the apostle's firm hope that, by God's grace, the church will stand firm to the last. We have here in a nutshell the contrast between the two dispensations.

For the apostolic church, the deliverance has taken place, the victory has been won.

Let us now look more closely at the text. In *vs. 12-13* Paul pays a great tribute to the Philippians: "As you have always obeyed." It is not clear whether Paul thinks of their obedience to God or, more specifically, of the way in which they have listened to him, Paul, and taken to heart his message, as from God. Since the concern of the apostle is the mutual relationship of the members of the church to one another, the obedience called for might be to the leaders of the community, specifically mentioned in *Phil. 1: 1.* This would explain the words, "Not only as in my presence but much more in my absence." Obedience was relatively easy so long as the apostle was with them, or at least kept in touch with them. But what about tomorrow? Would the party spirit triumph in Philippi as it had done in some other place? (See, for instance, *I Cor. 1: 10-17; 3: 16-23.*)

It is in this context that we must read the exhortation, "Work out your own salvation with fear and trembling." Is not the Philippians' temptation to be too self-assured? "Fear and trembling" is the attitude of one who knows his littleness and the greatness of God's calling. It is the fear and trembling Paul experienced when called to proclaim the gospel to the Corinthians (*I Cor. 2: 3*). It is the fear and trembling every preacher should feel when called to expound the Word of God. In the specific case of Philippi, the fear and trembling do not seem to concern the problem of individual salvation so much as the total life of the community, which a lack of corporate discipline threatens to destroy. But, of course, what destroys the life of the community threatens to destroy also the personal life of its members.

God's Grace and Man's Response

"Work out your own salvation with fear and trembling; *for God is at work in you,* both to will and to work for his good pleasure." (Italics added.)

What shall we make of this puzzling statement?

Those who insist on human freedom and initiative seize on the first phrase in the statement, whereas the staunch Calvinists insist on the second. Perhaps this sentence contains an ecumenical truth for us all.

All we are and all we do, we are and do by God's grace. This is not only stated here, it is part and parcel of Paul's message in all his letters. "For by grace you have been saved through faith; and this is not your own doing, it is the gift of God." (*Eph. 2: 8.*) But the proper character of grace is to call forth our response, of faith and love and obedience.

In Calvin's words:

"It is God that calls us, and offers to us salvation; it is our part to embrace by faith what he gives, and by obedience act suitably to his calling; but we have neither from ourselves." [1]

"The Holy Spirit, however, calls us to consider, that he wishes to work upon living organs, but he immediately represses arrogance by recommending *fear* and *trembling.* . . . For there is nothing that ought to train us more to modesty and fear, than our being taught, that it is by the grace of God alone that we stand, and will instantly fall down, if he even in the slightest degree withdraw his hand." [1]

---

[1] From *Commentaries on the Epistles of Paul the Apostle to the Philippians, Colossians, and Thessalonians.* Wm. B. Eerdmans Publishing Company. 1948. Used by permission.

"This is the true engine for bringing down all haughtiness—this the sword for putting an end to all pride, when we are taught that we are utterly nothing, and can do nothing, except through the grace of God alone." [1]

The very fact that the grace of God is at work in us should fill us with fear and trembling at the thought that our inertia, our self-sufficiency, our partisan spirit, might hinder the Holy Spirit in doing his work, thus delaying the building up of the church. Here lies the responsibility of the community as a whole and of every member of it. Because God is at work in Philippi, the Philippians are to be subject to one another, to work out their salvation. That grace does not excuse one from personal and corporate discipline is shown by Paul's own example (*I Cor. 9: 24-27*).

"Among Whom You Shine as Lights"

Up to now Paul has dealt mainly with the inner life of the church. Now, in *Phil. 2: 14-16,* he reminds the Philippians of their missionary vocation in the world that surrounds them. For Paul could never conceive a church that would not be missionary.

Nevertheless, the call to witness begins in a very matter-of-fact way: "Do all things without grumbling or questioning." How close this letter remains to everyday life and its petty troubles! We can easily imagine this little community, so similar is it to what we see elsewhere. The strong personality of the apostle is no longer there to animate and guide the common life. The appointed leaders (elders or "bishops," and deacons) have not the same skill and authority as the apostle; there is dissatisfaction as to their leadership in some quarters; some women feel important; there are little rivalries; there is a good deal of gossip going on in corners; all of this does not seem very serious, does it? But Paul thinks otherwise: "Do all things without grumbling or questioning, that you may be blameless and innocent, children of God without blemish in the midst of a crooked and perverse generation."

His is, first of all, a call for inner and outward discipline. Questioning may be all right at the right time and place; carried too far it paralyzes the common life and stifles all possibility of action. Paul is not requiring some moral perfection here. As a former Pharisee he knows the dangers of so-called perfectionism! What he is striving for is that humility, obedience, and forbearance one should find in those who are "in Christ," recipients of the same saving grace, called to the same service. This is the *condition* for their shining "as lights in the world, holding fast the word of life." To shine in a dark world, the church has to *be* the church, a new type of society whose style of life would be a challenge to the pagan society that surrounds her.

We have already stressed the fundamental character of such a community grounded "in Christ." The whole passage in *vs. 1-14* is nothing but a description of what it means to be such a community. Karl Barth has made some striking comments on this point:

"It is not the pharisaic ideal of being better than the wicked world, that Paul is proclaiming here. We need only keep always in view the fact that what distinguishes the Christians from the others is really nothing positive: it is in *fear and trembling* that they are something different from other men, in fundamental renunciation of the wish to be superior to other men. . . . As bearers of the Word of Life they ought indeed to shine, but the Word of Life is death to the poisonous germ of all self-glorification. That death is the shining light that becomes visible in them, the reflection of the light of Christ, in which they resemble the stars of the universe which illumine the night because they are themselves illumined by the light of day. By their complete lack of self-glorification, by living by grace and in fear and trembling, they represent without any special intention of doing so the order of God amid the disorders into which the unhumbled man daily falls and must fall—they are the breakwaters in the flood not by their Christian activity, propaganda, agitation and mission, but by their Christian existence." [2]

Not everyone would agree with Barth that humility is the *only* distinctive character of a Christian community, and we should take his statement with a grain of salt. But it is a healthy reminder of an all-too-often-forgotten truth. It is not his degree of achievement that characterizes the Christian, but the decisive encounter with Christ and the fundamental change of his esteem of himself and of his outlook on the world that this encounter provokes. Salvation by grace means that we cannot look down on anyone.

There is a striking similarity between portions of this chapter from Paul and the beginning of the Sermon on the Mount. The Beatitudes, in *Matt. 5: 1-12*, ascribe the Kingdom to "the poor in spirit," "the meek," "the merciful," "those who hunger and thirst for righteousness." It is to these humble people who depend upon God for everything that Jesus declares: "You are the light of the world. . . . Let your light so

---

[2] From *The Epistle to the Philippians*. John Knox Press. © SCM Press Ltd. 1962. Used by permission.

shine before men, that they may see your good works and give glory to your Father who is in heaven." What our Lord proclaimed, he lived. Conformity to his way of life is the key to the Kingdom.

This is the way in which the apostle wants to lead his beloved Philippians. His thoughts, as so often, turn to the day of Christ, that day when all the secrets of the heart will be uncovered and all men shall reap what they have sown. Will he, Paul, have been running in vain, or will his churches prove faithful to the very end? Will they be his "joy and crown" on that day of all days? So deeply does he hope this that he would gladly offer his life "as a libation upon the sacrificial offering of [their] faith" (*v. 17*).

The libation, in Jewish practice, was a drink offering, usually wine, which preceded or accompanied the sacrifice proper and was poured out to honor God. Paul's thoughts at this point revert to the possibility of martyrdom. His blood will be an offering of thanksgiving and praise. The text does not say clearly how this offering is related to the faith of the Philippians and to the consecration of their life to God. What Paul certainly believes is that his death as well as his life will be turned into a blessing for the churches entrusted to him. He and the Philippians share in the same priestly office, and in this both they and he should rejoice. Are not all of them called to offer their bodies as "a living sacrifice"? (*Rom. 12: 1-2.*)

There seems to be a contradiction between what the apostle says here and the firm hope he had expressed earlier in the letter (*Phil. 1: 25*). The issue of his trial remains an open question. Whatever his destiny may be, he stands with the Philippians in the same service, and the dominant note should be their common joy.

Christians Today, Note Well!

The problem of our Christian witness in the present world is often discussed. What kind of evangelism will carry weight in a society so involved in making money, in prestige and material success? The preaching of the church only reaches those who sit on the benches. Are deeds not more important than words? Are we, after all, any better than those outside the church fellowship?

The passage we have studied throws some light on these questions. We are reminded of the fundamental attitude Christians should have: first, no boasting about what we are or have, but rather a readiness to see the qualities of others, whether these are Christians or non-Christians. Secondly, to proclaim God's love, we have to demonstrate that love in our midst. We have to *be* that new kind of society built on mutual respect, forbearance, and love that will attract the outward world, a world caught in the plight of isolation and suspicion.

It is in that new type of relationship described in *Phil., ch. 2,* and *Matt., ch. 5,* in *being the church* that the "word of life" we proclaim may be heard by a world grown tired of "words, words, words."

8. FELLOW WORKERS IN THE LORD

(*Phil. 2: 19 to 3: 1*)

WE WERE FACED in the preceding passage with one of the deepest issues of Christian faith and life. Now Paul turns to practical questions, the sending of Timothy and the case of Epaphroditus. We are tempted to think that all this news is not very interesting, at least for us. But is not the tissue of everyday life made up of these little things, letters sent and received, illness and recovery, happy and unhappy relationships? Let us be thankful that this human side of the great apostle's life has been preserved for us. While being one of the greatest of the first-century theologians, he is, above all, a man of action, a missionary, a church builder. In this passage, as in all that came before, his dominant concern remains the welfare of the church.

"I Hope . . . to Send Timothy"

Paul's letter has slowly, tactfully, prepared the Philippians for the possibility that he might not come back among them. They should receive Timothy as an ambassador, invested with the apostle's authority (the word "send" has such an implication). We have seen that there were some tensions in the church; the apostle is evidently anxious not to let the situation deteriorate. Certain situations must be dealt with on the spot. Timothy is the only one to whom Paul could entrust such a mission. He will eagerly await his return. The one thing that can "cheer" the apostle in his ordeal is to hear that all goes well with his churches.

"I have no one like him, who will be genuinely anxious for your welfare. They all look after their own interests, not those of Jesus Christ." (*Ch. 2: 20-21.*) This is a sad remark, and one wonders what bitter experience lies behind it. Some commentators have suggested that Paul, after his long stay in jail, went through a period of depression. But the whole tone of the letter certainly does not sound depressed.

Men with heavy responsibilities unavoidably will go through moments of great solitude: there are many problems they have to carry alone, and very few people will understand what they are going through. If, according to the accepted tradition, the letter is written from Rome, the local church is not among those Paul has founded, and the remark made in *Phil. 1: 15* allows us to presume that not everybody in the church would appreciate the presence of so famous and cumbersome a prisoner. They had their own affairs to look after. Philippi was far away, and surely they had more important things to do than to go there.

But Paul's criticism goes deeper: this church does exactly what Paul urged the Philippians not to do; they are motivated by personal interests, not by the things pertaining to Christ and his Kingdom. This does not necessarily mean personal selfishness, although this may well be part of the picture. A local congregation can indulge in a kind of corporate selfishness; its main interest may lie in local prestige, the construction of a new church so that it has no money or thought left for the needs of the church at large. Christ's glory comes second to the little successes in which the church prides itself. His kingship over the world is lost sight of.

Paul, rightly or wrongly, feels that there is only one near him who shares his apostolic concern, his hopes and anxieties, and this is Timothy.

There must have been a very unique relationship between these two men. We have read how Paul met Timothy in Lystra and took him with him on his first trip to Macedonia and Greece. (*Acts, ch. 16.*) From then on we find Timothy in the picture at every turn of the apostle's life. He is to Paul like "a son with his father." Paul calls him his "true child in the faith" (*I Tim. 1:2*), his "beloved child" (*II Tim. 1:2*). He is Paul's faithful companion in all the hardships of apostolic travels; he is the trusted messenger one can send on delicate missions.

Paul's decision to send Timothy has been taken "in the Lord Jesus," and he will send him as soon as his own case is settled. Here again the hope is expressed that Paul may soon follow his messenger.

"Epaphroditus My Brother"

The case of Epaphroditus has given rise to many suppositions. Some would read between the lines that his mission had been a failure and that Paul was anxious in spite of this to assure him of a kind welcome. Some suppose he must have gone through a shipwreck; others that he had a nervous breakdown. Guesswork of this kind is always possible, but remains mere supposition. What is certain is that Epaphroditus had gone through a serious illness so that one feared for his life. Paul sees his recovery as a gift from God, who in curing him showed his mercy not only to the sick man but also to the heavy-laden apostle. Whatever the immediate cause of the illness, it befell Epaphroditus while he was engaged in the service of Christ and his church. Paul speaks warmly of him as a brother, a fellow worker.

Why, then, did Paul find it necessary to send him back? Epaphroditus, probably due to his state of health, seems to have felt homesick and nervous, worrying about the reactions at home. Paul decides to send him back, but does it in such terms that no one should be in doubt as to his appreciation of the services the man had rendered him and of his complete devotion to Christ's cause. There is a great deal of tact and love in the way in which Paul deals with what seems to have been a somewhat delicate situation. There are no "little things" for a true Christian where the happiness and peace of mind of a fellow worker are involved. In the world, great men would easily sacrifice the individual to "greater concerns." Not so in the church. This deep human quality in Paul shows even better than his most profound theological statements what it means to be a "complete Christian." It is "in the Lord Jesus" that the great apostle builds up the church in Philippi. It is also "in the Lord Jesus" that he deals with the case of Timothy or Epaphroditus.

"Finally, My Brethren, Rejoice in the Lord"

Why is this note of joy so constantly recurring in a letter written under the shadow of death? Is it that at such moments Christ's victory over sin and death takes on its deepest significance? The "farewell" of Paul is an appeal to look at the events of this life in the wider dimension of eternity. The joy of which Paul speaks here has nothing to do with earthly security or happiness. It has its source in God. Was it not a few hours before his arrest and execution that Jesus, according to John, speaks of his "perfect joy"? (*John 15: 11*.) It is the joy of a life freely offered. The sorrows and burdens of apostleship are part of such an offering. Paul relentlessly calls the church to share in this offering; because they partake of his priestly office in faith, in obedience, and through their gifts, they should also partake of his joy.

The sentence, "To write the same things to you is not irksome to me, and is safe for you" (*ch. 3: 1*), could be understood as a transition from what has preceded to a new theme (which, probably, to the Philippians is not so new). We should, rather, understand these words, however, as a conclusion to the exhortation in the two preceding chapters, as an apology for repeating things that the Philippians are supposed to know . . . and to practice.

One would expect the letter to end here. It seems that everything has been said. But suddenly a wholly new subject is broached.

9. IN THE POWER
OF HIS RESURRECTION

(Phil. 3: 2-11)

W<small>E HAVE ALREADY NOTED</small> the sudden change of
tone that occurs at this point in the letter.
Nothing in the preceding chapters had prepared us
for the passionate outburst of *v. 2:* "Look out for
the dogs, look out for the evil-workers." Is this a
fragment of a former letter, written in the heat of
the controversies between Paul and the Judaizing
Christians in the years 53–56? Or does Paul come
back, at this point, to a question he has already
dealt with earlier, but which he feels remains a per-
manent threat for the church? ("To write the same
things to you is not irksome to me," *v. 1.*) This is
a much-debated question, but a secondary one. It is
the content of the letter that matters most, and we
have here a basic statement of Paul's faith and a
precious reference to the personal experience of his
conversion.

The "evil-workers" mentioned here are evidently
not members of the church in Philippi, but outsiders.
They could be Jews, but given the hostility between
Jews and Christians at that time, it seems more plau-
sible that these "seducers" were Judaizing Christians.
We know from the letters to the Galatians and the
Corinthians that these people wanted to submit the
Gentile converts to the Jewish law, and particularly

to the rite of circumcision. They led an active propaganda campaign against Paul and threatened to destroy the faith and unity that existed among the churches.

The terms used by Paul are, therefore, of rare violence. There is a bitter irony in the term "dogs" applied to these men. It was the current word applied by the Jews to the Gentiles. The dog was an animal considered to be impure. For Paul, the impure ones are those who seek their salvation in the mutilation of the flesh. He does not take into account the fact that, for centuries, circumcision has been the outward mark of God's covenant with Israel, that it is sacred, therefore, to Jewish hearts. This would confirm us in the conviction that the adversaries are *not* Jews but men who claim to be Christians without having understood the radical incompatibility of the old practices with the new faith.

Jeremiah had proclaimed already that the true circumcision was that of the heart (*Jer. 4: 4*). Paul mentions three marks of the "true circumcision": it is to "worship God in spirit" or rather "by the Spirit of God" (ancient manuscripts differ on this point), to "glory in Christ Jesus," and to "put no confidence in the flesh."

The worship of the new people of God is a worship in spirit and in truth, the work of the Holy Spirit (*John 4: 23-24*), as over against the rites and ceremonies of the Old Covenant. The church does not glory in any ritual or moral achievements. Christ alone is her glory. By "the flesh" Paul always means the unredeemed man, not yet regenerated by the Spirit of God, who vainly tries to achieve his own salvation.

"I Count Everything as Loss . . ."

Here, suddenly, Paul starts expounding his own case. This is a fascinating bit of autobiography. If anyone, he says, could take pride in his human privileges, I could. Have I not been submitted to circumcision on the eighth day, according to Jewish rule? Am I not of the purest Jewish stock? I can prove my ancestry: I am a Benjaminite; I belong to that tribe which remained faithful to the Davidic monarchy to the last; I did belong to the strictest group of all, for I was a Pharisee. My zeal for the cause went so far that I persecuted the church. My obedience to the law was so strict that if anybody could be saved that way, I could.

And now comes the great confession: all these things he took pride in, he now counts as "rubbish." They are not only worthless, to be thrown away like garbage, they are a loss. "Paul is using the figure of a balance-sheet, showing Assets and Liabilities. All these advantages of birth and upbringing, he had formerly set down in the column of Assets; now he has transferred them to the column of Liabilities." [1]

Why this? On the Damascus road, the virtuous Pharisee suddenly found himself poor and naked, stripped of all his securities and self-righteousness, a murderer of God's elect. Paul discovered on that fateful day the meaning of salvation *by grace alone.* All his former efforts not only proved vain; they entertained in him the illusion that he could work out his salvation by his own means. How could he ever fall back under the bondage of the law?

---

[1] From *A Commentary on the Epistle to the Philippians*, by F. W. Beare. Harper & Row, Publishers, Inc. Copyright © 1959 by Francis Wright Beare.

Paul does not explain here *how* Christ entered his life. It is to be supposed that the Philippians knew the story. Paul has kept the burning memory of the time when he persecuted the church. (*I Cor. 15: 8-10; Gal. 1: 11-16.*) He insists that it is through God's direct revelation that he received the gospel.

How total and sudden the break with his former life was we can only guess. The privileged student sitting at the feet of the famous rabbi, Gamaliel, is to become an exile, forever banned from the fellowship of his former masters and fellows. The proud Roman citizen is to be treated like a vulgar tramp; the scholar is to earn his living as a tentmaker. He has lost his status among his own people; he has become a renegade of the faith of his fathers.

These are deprivations he counts for nothing because he has found Christ—or rather, *Christ has found him.*

We know in our day some men who have lost family, friends, and home country, and have risked their very lives for the sake of Christ. Such men know what it means to stake one's whole life on "Christ alone." The question arises in our minds: Would we be ready to lose all that in order to follow him? But the loss here is, above all, the loss of all self-righteousness. Saul of Tarsus was thrown off his pedestal of virtues and merits, thrown to the ground. We all have our little pedestals, and it takes a good deal of God's patient grace to break them to pieces. Paul had no righteousness left but *"the righteousness from God,"* no aim in life but to *know* "Christ Jesus my Lord."

Two Key Words

"Righteousness" is a key word in this passage. So is the word "know."

Righteousness is the condition of one who stands in a right relationship with God. In the Old Testament the *righteous* man is one who stands in a relationship of trust and obedience before God. God reckons Abraham as "righteous" because he believes God's promise and stakes his whole life on it. (*Gen. 15: 6.*) Abraham becomes the prototype of the believer in Paul's discussion of justification by faith. (*Rom., ch. 4.*) God's righteousness is shown in his faithfulness to the covenant of grace that he has made with his people. His aim is to restore a true relationship. It is his gracious will to reconcile us to him in Christ, *the Righteous One,* and to consider as righteous those who put their whole trust in Christ, in the power of his cross and his resurrection.

This is to say that the initiative lies with God. We can add nothing to what he has done for us in Christ, once for all. Only the empty-handed who "hunger and thirst for righteousness" will he fill with the joy and peace of his forgiveness. Faith is the act by which we respond to God's love and put our whole trust no more in ourselves and our "good works," but in Christ alone. Christ's coming puts an end to the law considered as a means of salvation.

This frontal attack against all the strivings of natural man, and also against the religious man of all times, could not be accepted easily by the zealous Jews who had worked hard all their lives to satisfy the requirements of the law. We should be aware that nothing is more difficult for human pride to accept than this blunt denial of all capacity to save oneself. Paul is aware of the stumbling block he places before men by taking so radical a position. But to him it is an "either-or," a matter of life and death. Only one could break the circle of sin and death in which mankind is enclosed. Only God's grace could open a way to freedom and life. To believe in our own works is like adding a bucket of water to the ocean and fooling ourselves into thinking that we have done something. It is the refusal to face the reality of our lostness. Therefore, the once-proud Pharisee now glories in his weakness, because it is in this very weakness that Christ's power will manifest itself:

"If I must boast, I will boast of the things that show my weakness." (*II Cor. 11: 30.*)

"For the sake of Christ, then, I am content with weaknesses, insults, hardships, persecutions, and calamities; for when I am weak, then I am strong." (*Ch. 12: 10.*)

"God chose what is foolish in the world to shame the wise, God chose what is weak in the world to shame the strong, God chose what is low and despised in the world, even things that are not, to bring to nothing things that are, so that no human being might boast in the presence of God." (*I Cor. 1: 27-29.*)

Could any saying challenge more bluntly the whole trend of our time than these affirmations of Paul? Has man ever been more conscious of his achievements, and, in some ways, rightly so? Are we not told that "man has come of age" and has learned to manage his own affairs? Are not the slogans of the day self-assertiveness, power, and success? woe to the weak? Does not Paul's message sound like the voice of Cassandra in a time of boom and prosperity? And yet, the question must be raised as to whether it is not such a radical message that our world needs. There is a good deal of doubt, emptiness, and even despair behind the outward self-assurance of modern man. All he does and strives for still ends in death. Does he not need more than ever the strong meat of the gospel of total lostness and total salvation?

The second crucial word of this whole message is "know." How does one *know* Christ "and the power of his resurrection"?

The verb is not frequently used in Paul's letters. We do find it *I Cor. 13: 12*, a passage that has a future reference: "Now I know in part, then I shall understand fully. . . ." In this same chapter Paul insists that love is greater than knowledge (*vs. 2-8*). Here knowing or knowledge seems to be taken in the Greek understanding of the word (*gnōsis*), meaning an intellectual apprehension of the truth.

In the letter to the Philippians, however, we think that Paul uses the word in the full meaning it had in the Hebrew Old Testament language: the whole person is involved in the act of "knowing." The thought of being known of God, in the depths of his being, filled the psalmist with awe (*Ps. 139*). For man, to know God is to do his will and to respond to his love, as the prophets of Israel proclaimed.

For Paul, to know Christ is to know him no longer according to the flesh of his earthly life, but as Savior and Lord (*Phil. 3: 7-11*); it is to know him in the power of his resurrection, as the conquerer over sin and death and all the powers that be. God has revealed this victory in raising Christ from the dead. We live in the faith that what Christ has done for us, he will do in us, transforming us into his likeness. But this implies a sharing "in his suffering."

Here again a question comes up: Is Paul thinking of the sufferings he has to go through for the sake of the gospel? Was not his life a constant "being

given up to death for Jesus' sake"? (*II Cor. 4: 11.*)
Was not his whole ministry as an offering for the
sake of those he calls from death to life?

Or is Paul thinking here of the death every Christian has to die, the death of the self-righteous ego
standing under the judgment of the cross? Of this
he says, elsewhere, "I have been crucified with
Christ; it is no longer I who live, but Christ who lives
in me" (*Gal. 2: 20*).

Both thoughts may be present in the apostle's mind.
The battle he carries on day by day is a consequence
of his having been baptized into Christ's death (*Rom.
6: 3-11*).

"That if possible I may attain the resurrection
from the dead." (*Phil. 3: 11.*) This "if possible"
might well disconcert and frighten us. If Paul is not
sure of his own resurrection, who could be? But the
point is that our earthly condition remains one of
hope, of complete dependence on God's mercy. We
are waiting for "the redemption of our bodies."
(*Rom. 8: 23-25.*) But Paul's hope is a firm hope.

"The saying is sure:
 If we have died with him, we shall also live with
 him;
 if we endure, we shall also reign with him;
 if we deny him, he also will deny us;
 if we are faithless, he remains faithful—
for he cannot deny himself."

(*II Tim. 2: 11-13.*)

10. RUNNING THE RACE

(*Phil. 3: 12 to 4: 1*)

PAUL is a fighter. He likes to draw his images from the games, or from the soldier's life. (*I Cor. 9: 24-27; II Tim. 2: 3-5.*) In *vs. 12-16* of *Phil., ch. 3,* he compares himself to a runner in the arena, all keyed up about the goal before him, looking neither right nor left, never turning round to measure the distance already covered, speeding on to win the prize.

One might think that the concept of salvation by grace alone encourages idleness: If God does everything, what remains for me to do? In fact, the opposite is a dynamic force that pushes one forward as nothing else could do. The love of Christ constrains us to throw ourselves wholeheartedly into his service. (*II Cor. 5: 14-15.*)

Paul has only one concern: to "know [Christ] and the power of his resurrection" and the fellowship of his sufferings. One might think that he is far ahead in all this. We know of the power of his ministry, of what he has suffered for the sake of his Lord. But he remains in all this the man with outstretched, empty hands who looks forward to the day of completion, to the resurrection from the dead. He has not yet reached "perfection." The Greek word may have been borrowed from the mystery religions. It does not describe a state of moral perfection but, rather,

a state of spiritual completion. Christ has taken hold
of his servant Paul. But Paul awaits the great day
of fulfillment. "For now we see in a mirror dimly,
but then face to face. Now I know in part; then I
shall understand fully, even as I have been fully
understood." (*I Cor. 13: 12*.) He awaits passionately
the day when his communion with Christ will be
complete, when he, Paul, the man of dust, will be
conformed to the man of heaven (*Rom. 8: 29; I Cor.
15: 49*).

The stress in this passage is on the *single-minded-
ness* of the runner. He never looks backward but
forward; he presses on. That this implies a great
deal of discipline Paul tells us elsewhere. (*I Cor.
9: 24-27*.) What does he mean by "forgetting what
lies behind"? Is he thinking of his former life? Or
does he refuse to measure the ground already covered? He reminds us here of the fundamental attitude of a Christian: no rehashing of past wrongs, of
past failures or successes.

Does this imply that Paul does not conceive of
any progress in Christian life? We do not think so.
He believes in the work of the Holy Spirit, in the
fruits of the Spirit; his own knowledge of Christ
has deepened as his ministry led him to share in his
master's sufferings. But what is all this compared
with the glory to come? And, anyway, it is the Lord's
work, not ours. Does not Christian experience tell
us that the closer we come to Christ, the more we
discover ourselves to be sinners, the more we have
to rely on his grace? This is why the apostle fixes
his eyes on him alone. The "upward call" or "high
vocation" is not here the specific ministry of the
apostle (*Phil. 3: 14*), but the Christian calling as
such. Therefore, Paul urges the Philippians, as ma-

ture Christians, to run with him toward the common goal, without allowing themselves to be disturbed by anything. But he is aware that they may not have come to the point where they could fully endorse his interpretation of the Christian life. He leaves it to God to open their minds and lead them on. "Only let us hold true to what we have attained." (*V. 16.*) (Or, "only let us 'stand in line' or 'march in line' at the point which we have already reached.")[1] The important thing is that they push forward, like one man, toward the common goal.

There must be no falling back from the point already reached. In saying this, Paul may well think of the troublemakers who in so many places have shaken the faith of the young churches. (See *Gal. 3: 1-4.*) We are responsible for keeping the faith, not for our degree of maturity or immaturity.

Paul displays here great pastoral wisdom. He does not attempt to force his convictions on people perhaps not quite ready fully to understand his line of thought. He trusts that God will lead them onward in due time. The important thing is that they remain faithful to what has already been revealed to them and press forward. Much harm has been done by Christians who tried to force others into the straitjacket of their own experience or their own system of thought, instead of waiting in patience and love for God's Spirit to do his work.

"Brethren, Join in Imitating Me . . ."

We have seen Paul's stress on humility. Is this phrase not betraying pride and self-consciousness?

---

[1] See *A Commentary on the Epistle to the Philippians,* by F. W. Beare. Harper & Row, Publishers, Inc. Copyright © 1959 by Francis Wright Beare.

It recurs several times in his letters. (*I Thess. 1: 6; I Cor. 4: 14-16.*) He admonishes his churches as a father would his children. In the particular case of the Philippians, it is clear that the example Paul sets before them is that of a man who rejects all self-righteousness and has only one aim in life: to know, to confess, to follow Christ.

Who are those who "live as enemies of the cross of Christ"? Commentators on the epistle disagree on this point. Some would insist (Karl Barth among others) that they are no other than the "dogs" mentioned in *ch. 3: 2*. They put their hope in the circumcision, "their god is the belly." They refuse the shame of the cross. Others (Beare among them) would object that Paul could not speak in such rough, disgraceful terms of the circumcision, which he had considered for so long as an ordinance from God. The argument seems strong, but Paul allows himself certain violences of language, as the passage in *ch. 3: 2* already showed. Yet, could Paul consider circumcision in itself as "a shame"? Is he not said to have circumcised Timothy himself, because he was born of a Jewish mother? (*Acts 16: 1-3.*) He could blame the Judaizers for refusing to put their whole trust in the cross of Christ; it is also possible that many of them, in maintaining the authority of the law, tried to save their status, to escape persecution and maybe the loss of their earthly goods.

Then some, following Calvin, would say that Paul had in mind here a larger group: all those who prefer the privileges and lusts of the present life to the shame of the cross. They glory in what is their shame; "their end is destruction."

Paul has stressed all along that it is through death that we attain life, the death of the self and all its

pretensions. Now he considers the opposite movement, the earthbound movement of self-assertiveness, which can only end in self-destruction. We are
reminded of Christ's words: "Whoever seeks to gain
his life will lose it, but whoever loses his life will
preserve it." (*Luke 17: 33; Mark 8: 35.*) The apostle
does not sit in judgment on these people, whoever
they may be; he thinks of them "with tears." His
apostolic heart bleeds; in rejecting "Christ crucified"
they have closed themselves to God's saving grace.

"But Our Commonwealth Is in Heaven . . ."

The word translated here as "commonwealth"
means the homeland, the political entity to which
one belongs. "We cannot have our 'hearts set on
earthly things, for' earth to us is alien territory."[1]
This interpretation of F. W. Beare hits the point.
Paul has developed elsewhere the thought that the
Christian's real abode is heaven: "Set your minds
on things that are above, not on things that are on
earth. For you have died, and your life is hid with
Christ in God." (*Col. 3:2.*) Our true citizenship
is in heaven. Similarly, we are told in I Peter: "Beloved, I beseech you as aliens and exiles to abstain
from the passions of the flesh." (*Ch. 2: 11.*) Again
Paul fixes the eyes of the church on the return of
her Lord, on that decisive day when we shall be delivered of "our lowly body."

Paul did not believe, as the Greeks did, and many
moderns tend to do, in the "immortality of the soul
as distinct from the body." He did believe in the bitter reality of death and in the resurrection "of the
body," meaning by this the whole person. Of course,
it would be a transfigured body. Christ's risen body
was different from the one he had on earth; so would
ours be. In I Corinthians Paul stresses the differ-

ence between a physical and a spiritual body. He uses
the similitude of the kernel and the grown-up plant.
(*I Cor. 15: 35-50.*) He does not try to remove the
mystery of this transformation. One thing he knows:
"Death is swallowed up in victory!" And this victory
is the victory of Christ over the power of sin and the
condemnation of the law. (*I Cor. 15: 54-56.*)

To Paul, faith in the resurrection is central. His
whole life is keyed to the manifestation of God's victory over all the powers of this world. In this ultimate
victory lies the meaning of the cross, the meaning of
history, the meaning of the existence of the church—
the meaning, also, of Paul's ministry with all its joys
and sufferings. The resurrection of Christ is the guar-
antee of our own resurrection: "If Christ has not been
raised, your faith is futile . . . . If in this life we who
are in Christ have only hope, we are of all men most
to be pitied" (*I Cor. 15: 17, 19*). Paul lives in the
expectation of the final redemption that will make all
things new: this is the goal toward which he runs.

The time between the resurrection of Christ and his
coming in glory is the time of the church, the time
when she too, like her Master, is called to a life lived
in the fellowship of his sufferings. Not only the individual believer, but the church as such, as Christ's
body on earth, stands under the cross and awaits the
time when the body of her humiliation will become
the glorious body of her risen Lord. Then the bride
will appear before him, "without spot or wrinkle"
(*Eph. 5: 27; Rev. 19: 7-8*), and the little community
in Philippi will be the apostle's "joy and crown." The
prize that the apostle covets, the crown of the victorious athlete for which he keeps running, is to present to his Lord at his coming a church that has
remained faithful and obedient to the end, a church
whose faith rests in Christ alone. (*Phil. 4: 1.*)

11. THE PEACE OF GOD

(*Phil. 4: 2-9*)

IF THOSE ARE right who see in *ch. 3* an insertion from another letter, the passage we study now would follow immediately the first sentence of *v. 1*. It would come as a natural conclusion to the main letter.

We have felt all along that there were some tensions in the church, although these were never specified. Now a particular case is mentioned, not to blame the two women involved, whose case was probably well known in the church, but to help them and to exhort others to help them. "I entreat Euodia and I entreat Syntyche to agree in the Lord . . ."

The wildest suppositions have been made as to who these two women were. Some have supposed that the names were allegorical and represented two conflicting parties in the church. Clement of Alexandria has suggested that one of them was Lydia and that she was Paul's wife. Paul speaks highly of them. They have "labored side by side" with him.

It is sometimes said that Paul had no understanding of women. But in this case, as in *Rom., ch. 16,* we find that he considered many of them as real and precious fellow workers and knew how to honor them. It appears that Euodia and Syntyche, for some unknown reason, found it difficult to work side by side. Perhaps their very zeal for the church had provoked some competition between them. Perhaps they had some conflicting views on church matters and got too excited about them. Such things happen.

Paul exhorts them to remain one "in the Lord." We have seen what this means for him. To be "in the Lord" is to be placed in that new situation where only one thing matters: the common service of the Lord in which all self-assertiveness, all spirit of domination, should be dead and buried. But Paul is also a realist; he knows how difficult it is for human nature to overcome certain feelings. He asks a trusted member of the congregation to help the two women to overcome their problems. In calling the man "true yokefellow," the apostle stresses his full trust in the man. We do not know who he was, nor do we know anything about the man called Clement. The name is Roman, and we know that Philippi was a Roman colony. Paul seems to mention here some faithful companions who have assisted him in the early times of the foundation of the church. Their names are written "in the book of life."

The thought of a book, or roll, in which the name of God's elect are written, is already to be found in the Old Testament. We have in *Ex. 32: 32* a moving cry of Moses, after Israel has committed a great sin: "But now, if thou wilt forgive their sin—and if not, blot me, I pray thee, out of thy book which thou hast written." In apocalyptic writings such as Daniel, the "book" becomes a record of God's judgment (*Dan., ch. 12*). Jesus tells his disciples they should rejoice that their names are written in heaven. (*Luke 10: 20.*) The term "book of life" is used frequently in the book of Revelation: *chs. 3: 5; 13: 8; 17: 8; 20: 12; 21: 27.* Only God knows those whose names are written in the book of life. But Paul has seen the Holy Spirit at work in his faithful companions and recognized in them the marks of their election. Possibly Clement, and the others not mentioned by name, have already passed away; they have died in the faith.

The whole concept of election is a difficult one. The thought that some have been chosen "before the foundation of the world" and others rejected is unbearable to most of us. It conflicts with our faith in Christ's all-embracing love, with the conviction that God "desires all men to be saved and to come to the knowledge of the truth" (*I Tim. 2: 4*). Our approach to this problem follows that which has been developed by Philippe Maury and Karl Barth. They argue that the thought of the New Testament on election is that "in Adam" we are all heading toward death, but that God in his mercy has predestined us from the beginning of time to find life in Jesus Christ. Yet the possibility of rejecting God's grace, of destroying one's soul, remains open. It has been rightly said there is one thing God cannot do: *force* us to love him! For this would be love no more. This is why Paul, at the same time, can rejoice in the firm hope of attaining fullness of life and exhort the Philippians to "work out [their] own salvation with fear and trembling."

"Rejoice in the Lord Always"

We have seen how constantly this note of joy recurs in this letter. The thought that he may never see his beloved church again seems ever present in the prisoner's mind. He wants the Philippians to look beyond the grave and to rejoice in their calling, whatever may befall him or them. He who really believes in God's grace knows a joy that no earthly power can take away.

"Let All Men Know Your Forbearance"

The term "forbearance" does not seem quite adequate. The same word is used in *II Cor. 10: 1* to describe "the meekness and gentleness of Christ." Christ is mild, as only one who holds all power can be mild: not on the defensive, not claiming his rights. The defensive attitude is always a sign of weakness, the reaction of one who feels threatened. The Philippians can be mild, forbearing, because "the Lord is at hand." Their right is in his hands, and they should fear no one. Paul's expectation is that the Lord will come soon. The first generation of Christians has eagerly expected this return to happen in its own lifetime, and Paul has certainly, to a certain point, shared this hope. (*I Thess. 4: 13-18.*) Now he knows that he may die before Christ's coming, but this coming remains the decisive moment when Christ's Lordship will be revealed to the whole world and he will vindicate his own. The question of time is not important: "with the Lord one day is as a thousand years, and a thousand years as one day" (*II Peter 3: 8*). "The Lord comes!" The end of history as a whole, and of every one of our little histories, is in his hand. This is what matters.

We all pray the Lord's Prayer, "Thy kingdom come, thy will be done, on earth as it is in heaven," but have we not lost the ardent longing of the early church: "Come, Lord Jesus! Maranatha"?

"Have No Anxiety About Anything"

Those who have put the Kingdom first in their lives do not need to be anxious about anything. Did not our Lord himself say so to his disciples? (*Luke 12: 4-7; Matt. 6: 25-33.*) Our worries often reveal a strange lack of perspective, a running after nonessentials as if they were tremendously important. Of course, there are certain anxieties which are legitimate. The Christian is not to display the indifference of the stoic; he has a heart of flesh which aches at the sufferings of others and is anxious to bring them relief. Christ's love makes us tender and sensitive to others' needs. But all this is to be brought before God in *prayer*. The opposite of anxiety is not indifference but *faith*. Paul is above all a man of prayer. Prayer is the secret force that enables him to face all the ordeals of his adventurous life, all the anxieties he goes through for all the churches, without ever being overcome.

But the dominant note of all prayer should be *thanksgiving*. We have noticed this already in the way Paul started his letter. He now makes it a rule of normal Christian prayer. We can put before God all our concerns. But it should be done in thankfulness. He who worries tends to forget God's grace, the mystery of his love as displayed in Christ, and all the gifts of everyday life. In other words, he tends to be ungrateful, to doubt God's power and mercy, to forget all that he has already received.

Trust God, lay all your problems before him, and the "God of peace" (*v. 9*) will give you his peace, a peace "which passes all understanding."

We have already seen in our study of *Phil. 1:2* the rich meaning of this word "peace" in Biblical language. The main thought is one of *wholeness,* a wholeness that man has lost and only God can restore in him; therefore, peace becomes synonymous with salvation. Peace is the characteristic of the Promised Land, of the Holy City (*Lev. 26:6; Isa. 52:7-10*), of the oncoming Kingdom. Peace is the order of God, in contrast with the disorder of the present world. Its source is in God. It is the normal state of being of the new creation man expects and longs for. Jesus Christ is "our peace" because, in him, God reconciled

the world to himself (*II Cor. 5: 17-20*) and made us
one through the power of the cross (*Eph. 2: 14-18*).
This is the peace that passes understanding, a peace
that man, by himself, could not conceive. It is the
peace that Jesus possesses, because of his perfect
union with the Father, and leaves as a parting gift to
his disciples. Such a peace is the first fruit of the
Spirit, a foretaste of the peace of the world to come.
It keeps watch over the church, it "guards" the hearts
and minds of her members so that they keep the unity
of faith and love and find their rest in God. Thereby
they are witnesses of God's order within the earthly
turmoil and strife.

It should be seen that Paul thinks first, in all this,
of the corporate life of the church. It is in our mutual
relation that the peace of God will be manifested as
a constructive and reconciling power. "Blessed are the
peacemakers, for they shall be called sons of God."
(*Matt. 5: 9.*)

Ruthless economic competition, will-to-power, racial and social tensions, national ambition are more
than ever dominant features of our world. Goodwill
is not enough to build up peace, even that very limited
coexistence that men call peace. The "sons of God"
may be called to sacrificial living. They must remember that he who came to serve and be our peace had
to go the way of the cross; this was the world's answer
to the Peacemaker. God's peace is of another caliber
and makes other demands on us than drafting some
resolutions or protesting against nuclear weapons. It
may mean for some risking their lives for others, being misunderstood and rejected. May the "peace of
God" preserve us from all false peace, peace that
would be an escape from reality, peace that would
abandon the world to all the power that is. It is a

prisoner for Christ's sake, whose whole ministry has been a relentless battle, who speaks of the "peace that passes all understanding" which should rule over all our thoughts and behavior.

The "final" exhortation of *v. 8* is somewhat unexpected. It sounds like a catalog of ordinary virtues. It has been said "that Paul here sanctifies, as it were, the generally accepted virtues of pagan morality." [1] Paul wants the Philippians to live in the world and to display the human qualities that any society would acknowledge (if not necessarily practice). This behavior is also part of the order of God.

Whatever is "true" probably here stands for truthfulness, straightforwardness; "honorable" would mean worthy of respect; "just" stands for equity in human affairs. The words "lovely" and "gracious" are interesting. In my own country of France the Huguenots are very virtuous but somewhat stiff people, whose dominant feature would not be graciousness. Paul wants the Philippians to be gracious people. He wants their thoughts to concentrate on all that is good, worthy of praise. He seems to say, "Be friendly, be kind, be human." Be "clean" in your thoughts and language. Do not cut yourselves off from the people among whom you are called to live; just be yourself— a self, of course, that has in God the source of its being. Here again Paul sets himself as an example: the Philippians have been instructed by him in what they should do, and they have accepted his teaching; they have seen him live. All this they should remember, now that he is no more among them. They should remain faithful to what they have already received.

---

[1] From *A Commentary on the Epistle to the Philippians*, by F. W. Beare. Harper & Row, Publishers, Inc. Copyright © 1959 by Francis Wright Beare.

Paul does not speak here as an individual, but with the authority of an apostle, as the voice of the church of God.

"What you have learned and received and heard and seen in me, do; and the God of peace will be with you." (*Ch. 4: 9.*)

12. FREEDOM AND MONEY

(Phil. 4: 10-23)

THE LETTER seemed to come to an end, but suddenly Paul starts again on a new subject: the gifts sent by the Philippians to the apostle. These thanks come strangely late in the letter, especially in view of the fact that they have been brought by Epaphroditus, whose visit and departure have already been mentioned earlier. We know that the Philippians have heard of the man's illness, so that some messenger must have gone to Philippi since his arrival. For all these reasons, we would side with those who believe that we have here an earlier "letter of thanks" (see Chapter 1).

Paul has certainly a way of his own in which to thank his benefactors. He rejoices *"in the Lord"* that the Philippians should have found this occasion to show their faithful concern for him, for his apostolic ministry. But he wants them to know that he would have managed even without their gift. This passage gives us an insight into Paul's attitude toward money, but shows also how anxious he is to preserve his independence.

That Paul rejoices "in the Lord" means that here, as always, his gratefulness goes first to God and secondly to those God has used as instruments of his mercy. The Philippians have been able "at length" to fulfill their desire to help him, to let their concern "blossom anew" or "put forth fresh shoots." Paul makes clear that they are not responsible for the delay. He is not complaining about the difficulties of his situation, about his poverty, because he has learned to be content in any situation; the word he uses conveys an idea of independence, of freedom, and seems borrowed from the philosophical language of the Stoics. But Paul's attitude has nothing to do with the kind of detachment that philosophy implies. He knows "how to be abased" (the idea here is not only of material poverty but of humiliation, the word he uses in *Phil. 2:8* when speaking of Christ). He knows also how to live in plenty. This is his *freedom*. He can endure hunger and want, and he can enjoy earthly goods when they come his way. No asceticism in all this, no thought that any merit could be attached to poverty. His independence toward the conditions in which he has to live has its foundation in his total dependence on him who sends him. The Lord's strength manifests itself in the servant's weakness: "for when I am weak, then I am strong" (*II Cor. 12: 10*). His whole confidence lies in the promises and the faithfulness of God. God's power has no limits, and the life of his apostle is solely in his hands.

"Yet It Was Kind of You . . ."

It was "good," or "right" for you "to share my trouble" or "my tribulations." The word is a strong one. Paul thinks of all the hardships of his apostolate and of the fact that the church enters into a kind of partnership with him through her gifts. He has not forgotten what the Philippians have done for him earlier, when he left them after having preached the gospel to them for the first time. He reminds them that their case has been quite exceptional. They are the only church with which he has ever kept a running account. They sent him money twice while he was still in Thessalonica. The phrase seems to imply that they went on doing so after that, until, for some reason, the sending was interrupted.

Why is this church the *only one* from whom Paul ever accepted money? The remarks he makes elsewhere on this money problem throw some light on what he says here: to accept material help from this church reveals a unique relation of trust and partnership. Paul seems to have made it a point, all through his apostolic ministry, not to be supported by those he evangelized. We are told that on arrival in Corinth he earned his living as a tentmaker (*Acts 18: 2-3*). He writes to the Corinthians that he would have been entitled to receive his food and drink, as others did. "Who serves as a soldier at his own expense? Who plants a vineyard without eating any of its fruit? Who tends a flock without getting some of its milk?" (*I Cor. 9: 7.*) Had not our Lord himself sent his disciples without any money, so that they should depend on the hospitality of the towns they visited? (*Luke 10: 5-7.*) Paul does not question that this is the normal rule, but he "boasts" that he has made use of none of these rights. He is compelled to preach the gospel; his sole privilege is to deliver his message *"free of charge"* (*I Cor. 9: 18*). Surely he does not do this to acquire some "merit." He probably gives us the key to his attitude when he speaks of enduring anything "rather than put an obstacle in the way of the gospel of Christ" (*v. 12*).

In his missionary situation, exposed to the suspicion, or even open attack, of the Jews, and to the hostility of pagan surroundings, he would not have it said that he preached the gospel for the sake of

money. He writes to the Thessalonians that his preaching has never been "a cloak for greed" (*I Thess. 2:
5-9*). He wants to avoid any misunderstanding as to
the disinterested way in which he preaches the gospel,
as over against the false preachers who seem to have
worked on other terms (*II Cor. 11: 7-15*). The fact
that his enemies easily used slander forces Paul to
specify that the Macedonians are the only ones to
have ever supported him. That they were both poor
and generous we know from another beautiful testimony he renders to them in the same letter (*II Cor.
8: 1-5*). It is because the Philippians have given their
hearts to the Lord and to his service that Paul *can*
accept their gifts. These are written down to their
credit in heaven. Paul is now fully supplied, but he
rejoices less in his need being covered than in the
fact that such a gift of love is a well-pleasing and
fragrant offering to God. As God covered Paul's need
in sending Epaphroditus to him, so will he cover the
needs of the Philippians, "according to his riches in
glory in Christ Jesus." Paul probably does not think
so much here of material goods as of all the blessings
the church receives "in Christ Jesus." To God alone
all praise should go. This is the meaning of the solemn
doxology the apostle uses as a conclusion: "To our
God and Father be glory for ever and ever."

Money Problems

What can we learn from this "letter of thanks"
about the Christian's attitude toward money? It is,
first of all, an example of Christian *freedom*. Because
Paul is entirely in the service of his Lord, he need not
worry about the morrow. He lives the reality of the
saying of Jesus: he who seeks first the Kingdom of
God need not be anxious about his daily life (*Matt.*

6: 25-33). But this does not prevent the apostle from earning his living and working hard. It does not mean that he has not had to face dire poverty. But all this has been lived "in the Lord," endured for his sake. Wealth, as well as poverty, is to be received "in the Lord," enjoyed as his gift. Neither poverty nor wealth is important, but receiving what comes, day after day, from God's hand. This is freedom.

Let us recognize that such freedom is easier for a man who has no family to care for! But its source lies deep down in the seriousness of our commitment and of our prayer life. Our time is so absorbed by making money that Christians have a specific witness to render in this realm. Financial interests dominate so many lives today that it is urgent for the church to practice a certain detachment from earthly power and wealth and to stress the need for sharing these goods with the less privileged sections of our human society. Is it not an interesting fact that these kinds of questions came up many times at the recent sessions of the Vatican Council?

What shall we say about Paul's insistence that he would rather earn his living than be paid for preaching the gospel? This he considers as an element of his freedom. He is careful not to generalize his case and certainly does not set a rule. Interestingly enough, some men in our own time are struggling with a similar problem. They discover that a paid minister will not succeed in establishing normal contacts with certain "unchurched" people, partly because their way of life is too far from his, partly because he is "paid to say such things." The example of the "worker priests" and of other new attempts to bridge this gap seem to show that new forms of ministry are needed. The witness of a layman engaged in the same work will carry more weight with the non-Christian than that of the clergyman. This does not mean that we shall not go on needing full-time pastors and teachers.

Paul's freedom had been costly. No one could force him to preach another gospel than the one that his Lord himself had entrusted to him. He went from conflict to conflict with his own people, with the secular society fearing for her interests (recall the story of his arrest in Philippi and the riot in Ephesus), with the state which does not like "troublemakers."

In our troubled times, men and women have been called to suffer for that same freedom of the gospel, and others will follow the same road. To them, too, Paul might say: "My God will supply every need of yours according to his riches in glory in Christ Jesus." (*Phil. 4: 19.*)

"Greet Every Saint . . ."

The two last verses of this epistle are farewell greetings, not only from Paul, but from one church to another. The greeting goes to "every saint" in Philippi, to all those who are in Christ Jesus. The remark has been made that the apostle, in this letter, finds it necessary to stress again and again that *all* members of the church are included in his prayers, in his offering, in his longing for them. The letter is probably sent to the leaders of the church, but should be shared with all. And the "saints" of the church at Rome (or Caesarea, or Ephesus?) join in the greeting, "especially those of Caesar's household."

This mention of Caesar's household immediately makes one think of Rome. We can imagine the apostle telling his guardians about Christ and the military guard talking about this strange prisoner and the good news spreading in the very stronghold of the

Empire. But there were praetorian guards in cities like Caesarea, Ephesus, and Philippi. Anyway, it is among Roman soldiers that Paul at that moment has found the keenest openness to his gospel. These soldiers have become "saints in Christ Jesus." They *care* for their brethren in Philippi. They have heard about the marvelous commonwealth of the church that knows of no frontiers.

"The Grace of the Lord Jesus Christ Be with Your Spirit"

The first words of the letter were "grace" and "peace." We have already commented upon these two words. Are they not the keynote of the whole letter? Paul's ardent plea for unity, for steadfastness, for humility, flows out of his response to God's grace, to the mystery of his freely offered, unfathomable love, as revealed in Christ. It is to this active love that Paul now commends the spirit of the Philippians—their minds, their hearts, their whole being. It is his final blessing.